Jacques Abbadie

Chemical Change in the Eucharist

In Four Letters Shewing the Relations of Faith to Sense

Jacques Abbadie

Chemical Change in the Eucharist
In Four Letters Shewing the Relations of Faith to Sense

ISBN/EAN: 9783337113131

Printed in Europe, USA, Canada, Australia, Japan

Cover: Foto ©Lupo / pixelio.de

More available books at **www.hansebooks.com**

Chemical Change

in the

Eucharist.

In four letters chewing
the relations of faith to
sense, from the French
of Jaques Abbadie, by
John W. Hamersley, A.M.

In vain do they worship me, teaching for doctrines
the commandments of men.—MATT. vii. 7.

LONDON:
SAMPSON LOW, SON, AND MARSTON,
MILTON HOUSE, LUDGATE HILL.
PUBLISHED FOR THE EDITOR.

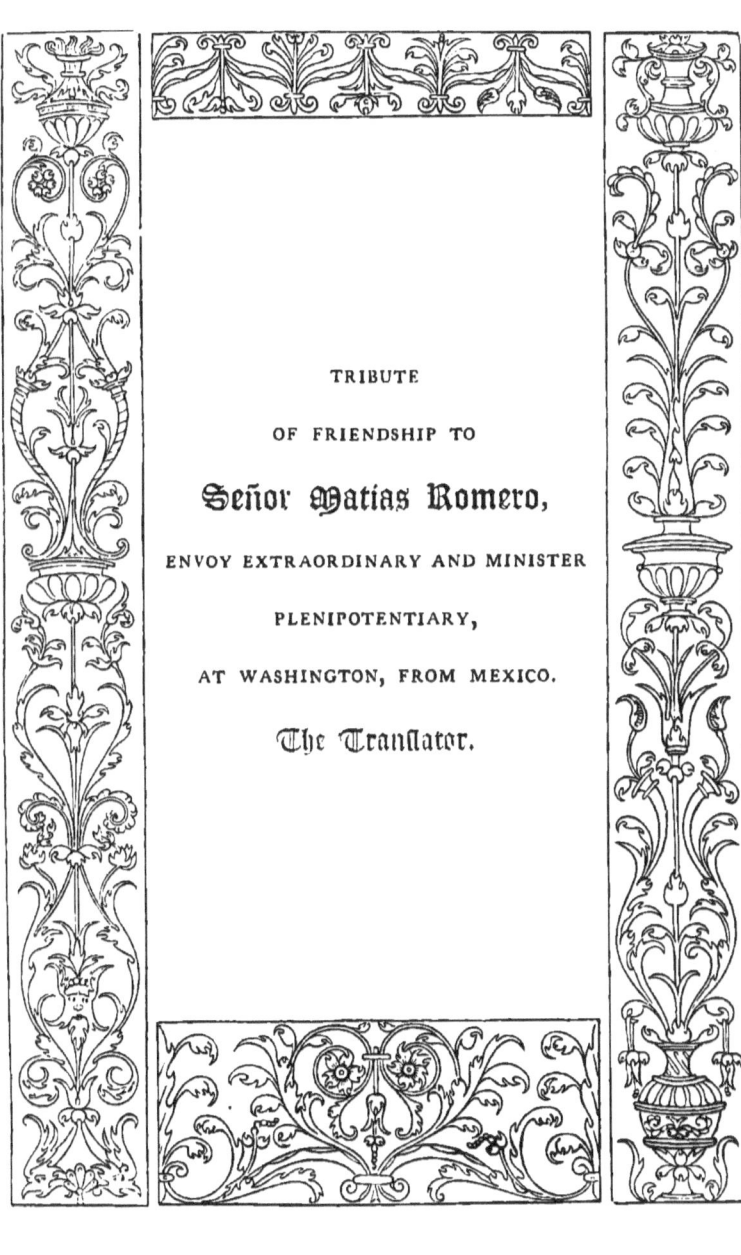

TRIBUTE

OF FRIENDSHIP TO

Señor Matias Romero,

ENVOY EXTRAORDINARY AND MINISTER

PLENIPOTENTIARY,

AT WASHINGTON, FROM MEXICO.

The Translator.

Tranſlator's Preface.

 HE deſign of Louis XIV. to commit Turenne to the Roman creed gave the firſt impulſe to the controverſy that cloſed with theſe cauſtic letters of the Dean of Killaloo.

Louis, by inſtinct, bigot and deſpot, tempted the ambition of the chief captain of the age.

The politic Port Royaliſts ſent the Marſhal a theſis, charging the actual preſence on the Proteſtant faith, and change of faith to be impoſſible.

Anne de Nompar, his wife, an ardent Calviniſt, doubting the ſtability of her huſband, he ſurviving her, induced Claude, the great polemic of France, to expoſe the fallacies of Port Royal.

The cordial reception, by the Roman laity, throughout

Europe, of Claude's *Critique*—written on a journey from Languedoc to Montauban, circulated only in manuſcript— evoked the able work of Arnauld and Nicole,—*La Perpétuité de la foi dans l'égliſe catholique ſur l'Euchariſtie.*

Claude replied: Arnauld rejoined: Nouet, the Jeſuit, came to the relief of Arnauld, in the *Journal des Sçavans:* Claude anſwered Nouet in the Provincial Letter that called out two more folios from Arnauld, which Claude met with equal ability and learning. A clique of the Janſeniſts, ſecretly pleaſed with the confuſion of Port Royal, yet bound in honor to appear in the liſts, iſſued their *Juſt prejudices againſt Calviniſm:* Claude reviewed it in his maſterly *Défenſe de la Réformation.*

Abbadie's iron pen, ever nibbed with mercileſs courteſy, now the maſſive mace of Richard, now wary and keen as the Saracen's cimetar, gave the *coup de grace* to the Papal hero of the clerical tilt. Our author was born in the Canton of Berne, 1654: he ſtudied at Saumur, was doctorated at Sedan and inſtalled Paſtor of the French church of Berlin at the inſtance of Count d'Eſpence.

He left his paſtorate to follow the fortunes of Marſhal

Schomberg ; in Holland, they joined the Prince of Orange in his Britiſh *coup d'Etat* of 1688.

After the death of Schomberg, who fell in the battle of the Boyne, Abbadie was preſented to the benefice of the Savoy, London, and ſoon after, preferred to the Deanery of Killaloo, Ireland : he died in 1727.

His *Traité de la Verité de la Religion Chrétienne,* won the applauſe of all Chriſtian ſects, and ſtill ſerves as a rich armory to the Church.

The ſimple queſtion raiſed at Port Royal, had involved the entire Latin dogma ; *that every atom of the elements, by conſecration, is changed into the natural body, ſoul, and divinity of the Son of God, and to the blood that flowed from his ſide ; that very body, born of a virgin, that hung upon the croſs, roſe from the dead, and ſits at the right hand of the father.*

To this teſt of faith, Rome is pledged no leſs by the decrees of Lateran and Trent, than by the blood of that noble army of martyrs *who had not ſo learned Chriſt.*

She enforces it by threats of damnation, and ignores all doctrine uncovered by the concurrence of the Apoſtles, the

Fathers and the Church, at all times and in all places : in her own terſe language, *ſemper, et ubique, et ab omnibus creditum.*

The ſubjeĉt derives a ſpecial intereſt from the Quixotry of her appeal to ſcripture, which in waiving the frequent aegis of tradition from her moſt offenſive and leaſt tenable tenet, expoſes a tendon-Achilles to the jeſt of the flippant, the ſhafts of wit and the ſcorn of reaſon.

Probable idolatry inveſts the queſtion with yet a deeper intereſt ; for if the dogma is not true, and the Roman latriant juſtified by intention : intention atones all idolatry, as all idolaters worſhip God in his image or in his works.

If the dogma is true, and by failure of intention of the Prieſt, the bread is unchanged to the living God, or ſhould a defiant doĉtrine, adopted on credit, prove falſe, is the Catholic idolater ſecure in the ſponſorſhip of his Church, or in the funded merits of her ſaints? No faĉts in hiſtory are more tangible than its birth, growth and canonical adoption.

Like the figment of Purgatory until the Council of Florence, and the immaculate conception of our own day, this monkiſh bantling was joſtled, *de opinione*, until *vox ecclefiae* was forced to affiliate or ignore it.

The Fathers, indeed, exalted the efficacy of the ſupper : they hallowed the ſignificants by names of things ſignified, and aſcribed to the bleſſing a myſtic virtue, conſonant to Anglican teaching : yet the elements retained their normal eſſence, and were tranſubſtantiated into our fleſh, the living ſacrifice: that, in the language of St. Auguſtine, *neither truth may be wanting in the Sacrament, nor Pagans have occaſion to make us ridiculous for drinking the blood of one ſlain.*

The idol Schiſm of the eighth century, determined the Greek doɛtrine.

The Seventh Ecumenical Council at Conſtantinople, A.D. 754, unanimouſly condemned the worſhip of images : their decree ran :—*the Savior having left us no other image of himſelf, but the Sacrament, in which the ſubſtance of the bread is the image of his body, we ought to make no other image of our Lord.*

The Second Council of Nice, in 787, annuls the aɛt of Conſtantinople, affirming *the Sacrament after conſecration to be properly Chriſt's body and blood; not the image and antitype.*

This was the firſt official notice of the carnal preſence:
Rome trod in the ſteps of Greece.

Paſcaſius Ratbert, a Benediĉtine monk, A.D. 831, was
the firſt to give the novelty its odious form and prominence
in the weſtern Church; it made him Abbot of Corbey,
provoked a ſharp confliĉt with Abbot Frudegard, a prompt
rebuke from the Scholiaſts, and ſevered him from his abbey.

Paſcaſius was anſwered by the learned Ratram, his
ſubordinate, by the Biſhop of Auxerre, and by Scotus, the
father of ſcholaſtic divinity, all of them living and dying in
Roman communion; ample proof that the change of ſubſtance was not then organic law: *we oppoſe this error*, ſaid
the Archbiſhop of Mentz, *with all our might.*

In the eleventh century, it is ſtill an open queſtion.

Berenger, archdeacon of Angers 1059, by *diĉtation* of
the Council of Rome, Nicholas II. preſiding, abjures the
figure in form of execration againſt all *who deny the true
body and true blood of our Lord to be veritably and ſenſibly
handled and broken by the Prieſt, and veritably and ſenſibly*
GROUND BY THE TEETH OF THE FAITHFUL.

Nicholas ſends the glad tidings of the redemption of the

Church from ſcandal, throughout Italy, Gaul, Germany and wherever the error had reached. Berenger, eſcaped from the Council, forthwith retracts his abjuration, on the ground of coercion.

This feature of the creed ſeems to be canonically tranquil for twenty years, although the Church has detected a *pravity of Berenger*, and doubts that his diction, unleſs carefully rendered, may ſavor of the leaven of hereſy, *in making parts of Chriſt's body.*

Berenger is cajoled by a ſafe conduct of Gregory VII. to the Sixth Council of Rome, 1079: he and others boldly advocate the figure.

A minority of the 150 Biſhops, after a ſharp ſtruggle, yield to the majority vote. Berenger, in fear of perſonal ſafety, revokes the retraction of his abjuration, and again relieves the anxiety of the Church, by defining the faith in a ſounder form of words, to wit: the creed of Nicholas, and his Council of 113 Biſhops, amended by *judicious omiſſions:* all which Berenger repudiates by manifeſto, when ſafe in France.

The manner of the Euchariſt, apparently quieted at

Lateran, is bitterly conteſted after the lapſe of three centuries, between the Dominicans and Franciſcans at Trent,
the laſt general council of the Roman Church—the nuncio
Verona's compromiſe reſolution directs, *the uſe of as few
words as poſſible, and terms ſufficiently general to meet the
views of both.*

It is a grave thought that a ſection of Chriſt's flock,
retaining traits by which Proteſtants might profit, ſometime,
champion of the oppreſſed, the kebla of learning, the altar
of ſacred art, cheriſhing at the meridian of ſcience, the
ſtagnant policy that perſecuted Galileo, libels *public ſchools
as public peſts, and liberty of conſcience as the liberty of per-
dition.*

Still more ſad, that a Church embracing within her pale
ſo many, with whom—through the mercies of unpromiſed
grace—we truſt to tabernacle in the ſpirit land : pretends
to do what God cannot do ; create again the ineffable, ſelf-
exiſtent I AM the uncreated creator.

Pagans, it is true, carve and worſhip their Gods, and can-
nibals eat their fellow-man : yet, in the annals of time, nay,
in the fancies of fable, none but the devotees of Mary and

her Son, *animated with a firm hope, penetrated with a lively faith, inflamed with an ardent charity,* in an unknown tongue, chaunt a cruſt, into the body, ſoul and divinity of their Maker and Redeemer, adore and ſwallow him.

Yet theſe are they, that claim excluſive right to wear the ermine of reaſon, and to bear the veſſels of the Lord.

Had anathema dominion of thought,ocean would not wed ocean with the iron ring, nor vapor ſweep the whirl-wind—lord of ſpace—nor ſcience, atteſt Jehovah's glory, and her holy miſſion, with the records of the rocks : nor range the ſkies, to map the mazes of a thouſand worlds, nor forge the bolts of heaven into bonds of Chriſtian love, pealing hoſannas over zones, flaſhing pæans through the floods, thrill the planet with a common pulſe.

The piety of the Propaganda would be exhauſted in the cruel artifice of tenors, the baptiſm of bells, the torture of heretics, the benediction of horſes and aſſes, and in hawking the mercies and manſions of another world.

When deſpotiſm was ſecure in ignorance, her ſpecious ceremonial, her menacing oubliette and thumb-ſcrew could ſhape the creed of the *Sabot ;* now, the ſullen pupil of reform taught that the *world moves,* ſpite of councils and curſes, renews her overtures to the ſenſe of ſight.

Who can forbear a ſmile at your viſible miracles, your winking and weeping madonnas, your fluxing the clotted blood of Januarius, your foreſts of *Vera Crux?* If thoſe *fruits of ſanctity* are not impoſtures to magnify the prieſt, give us a ſounder word.

Are your inviſible miracles leſs preſumptuous? if wiſer than Omniſcience you ſubvene his polity by fraud, are you Lord of Omnipotence, that you degrade the infinite to the finite—ſpeak into re-exiſtence him that ſpake and it was done, and multiply and ſacrifice in countleſs millions, him *that holdeth the waters in the hollow of his hand, him that inhabiteth eternity?*

The Incarnation of the maſs, that filches the miracles from Chriſt, the fouleſt ſtain of the Roman hereſy, her ſtake and fagot ultimatum; a living ſpring of laxity within, and defection from her fold, is the *great gulf,* that ſunders the unreformed from the univerſal church; a putrid corpſe chained to St. Peter's Keys.

You refer us to your own authority, we refer you to Patriſtic
authority, and to the author of authority: if you abide by
Holy writ, Abbadie tries the iſſue by the ordeal to which
Chriſt and his apoſtles aſſigned it.

The Latin bride of Chriſt, *overſhadowed by the power of
the moſt high;* pliant, at her need or choice, wanton and vin-
dictive where ſhe dare—*united*—unchurched by our Eaſtern
mother, ignored by the Britiſh Church planted in perſon by
the apoſtles, repudiated by her ſiſter of Avignon; frantic
anathemas bandied between rival popes; councils wrangling
with councils, councils with Popes—*Apoſtolic*—her Prelacy
brawling, ſordid and profligate—her Hierarchs, *ſervi ſervo-
rum Dei,* always arrogant; vicars of Chriſt, not ſeldom impious and infamous—her creed; *the ſame to-day, yeſterday
and forever,* ſhifting with the wind—her mangling and
ſhackling of Scripture—her cloiſtered and clerical celibacy;
its terrific reaction; her denial of Chriſt, preſaged in thoſe
ſtartling words, *what have I to do with thee?* her uſurpation
of the Godhead; her aſſumption of tranſomnipotence—*unerring;* a millennium of ſchiſm, pollution, ſubterfuge and
crime ſuperſcribed with God's name, had nerved the

Tranſlator's Preface.

Chriſtian world for the fiat of the firſt bold ſpirit that dared confront power with truth.

Time is the crucible of Juſtice; divine rights are merged in ſong and ſtory; Pontiffs and Princes reign by the grace of the maſſes.

Chriſt's nuncios conferred and revoked crowns in heaven and on earth. Spain alone, the only Chriſtian harbor of the ſlaver, offers an aſylum to Pius, the only living Sovereign, Chriſtian or Pagan, that has given *language to ſympathy* with human bondage.

By the laws of reaction, Germany is ſceptical, France, infidel; the Papacy of Ireland, the price of her blood, independence and proſperity, but an ulcer of Saxon hate.

Millions of Fenians brave Pope and prieſthood; Scandinavia, Holland, Pruſſia, loathe their mediæval huſks; the ſceptre of Europe is Proteſtant by edict of the needle gun; the dry bones of Chili, Brazil, Peru, live at the touch of progreſs; Mexico has faith in freedom.

Italy, the cradle and grave of bigotry, has enfranchiſed the word of God, and the voice of nature; Dominican cells, inquiſitors' dens, ring with the clarion tones of Gavazzi; conventual mortmains are ſecularized, vows of chaſtity are voidable, clerical marriage, a civil contract; *the Carbine, her Goſpel.*

The ſucceſſor of Peter, victim of the ſucceſſor of Pepin, donor of Peter's patrimony, the tribute of Pepin's uſurped crown of France; vice-gerent of God, omitted at ſecular councils, ſtripped of his *kingdom of this world*, his paſtoral imprecations recoiled, ſheathes his vicarial ſword by command of his earthly maſter.

Such are the repayments of divine vengeance—the fall of Rome conſecrates the hereſy of Luther.

No one who heeds the leſſons of paſt, or paſſing hiſtory, can doubt, that Papiſm lacks but the power to procruſt all diſſidents to Theophagian rule; *the ſame to-day, yeſterday and forever.*

It is no idle fear, that the ſacred college has final views in the United States, a prize worthy her traditions; the hundred millions that will tread that ſoil in half a century, will awe the world, for good or ill.

We diſtruſt that ſudden *ſolicitude for the welfare of four millions of liberated Africans,* whoſe liberation Romaniſts oppoſed ; ſtill more, thoſe *faithful ſhepherds* poſted on the prairies, to *proteɡ̌t the Chriſtian flock, expoſed to the incurſions of mercenaries and the ravages of wolves.*

It may be a Napoleonic idea, in virtue of his temporal vicariate, at once to cut the Papal knot, avenge the preſtige of France, ſullied by his Mexican fiaſco, and reſtore aſcendancy to the Latin race, by ſhifting to theſe *partes infidelium,* the Political See, the Anachroniſm, the Soleciſm, the nuiſance of Europe.

Our ſtern hybrid of Puritan and Huguenot, ſtill tolerant, even of intolerance, is watchful of ambitious faith ; face to face with civil and ſpiritual liberty, Romaniſm will be deromanized—the Papal upas will wilt in a free ſoil.

May theſe crumbs thrown on the waters in the ſpirit of charity and peace, attraɡ̌t the candor and manhood of the Roman laics with whom we muſt live, and would not claſs *imperium in imperio.*

Your own records verify all our faɡ̌ts ; you are conſcious of the Papal chill at the Proteſtant hearth, you cannot doubt that loyalty to your Church is treaſon to your flag.

You know that both ſexes and all ages kneel to celibate foreign officials, not yet canonized, never republican, *in loco Dei;* who, in privacy of penitent and prieſt ; ſecrecy, guarded by the curſe of Rome; ſecrecy, above the law ; ferret the unguarded thoughts we dare not confide to man, or bluſh to confeſs in prayer.

You know your altars in our eyes, reek with Jeſuit peſti-lence ; with blood of Albigenſes. How my pen quivers with the cry of the Vaudois, hounded to the flaming pen—the wail of ſtrangling infancy—the ſtifled groans of blood-ſmeared hoary heads—the martyr's prayer—*let not this be laid to their charge*—hark—that agonized ſhriek, courſing the heart-throb of ſix hundred years—the mother in the gorging holocauſt, appeals with charred hands to the God of vengeance ; the frantic daughter, vainly ſtruggling from the Catholic Satyr's clutch, to purge her ſhame in the embers of her mother's breaſt.

Maidens under vows to charity and mercy, transformed by one taſte of blood from foſſiled ſweetneſs to furies, with gnaſhing teeth, ſwell the *Veni Creator* of the army of the Croſs, inſpired by ſaints Dominic and Francis, led by mailed prieſts, ſent and abſolved by Innocent III. now with ſurplus righteouſneſs, mediators for your ſins before the throne of Grace—Oh, God ! how weak are words to paint that carnival of hell !

Is it a marvel that good men were ſtung to mad revenge ? Is it a marvel that every Latin ſpire, in our eyes, is a plague ſpot to its vicinage, a beacon of craft and deluſion, of blaſphemy, turpitude and tyranny, lurid with the problem of the future ?

Is it a marvel that Bible Chriſtians, grateful to the wardens of the oracles—albeit, living monuments of prophetic truth, divine wrath and their own ſhame—can eaſier condone the honeſt, unobtruſive negation of Iſrael, than the inſolent aggreſſion of profanity ?

Is it a marvel that the ban of ſocial leproſy goads the ſenſitive Papiſt to bigotry or infidelity ?

We ſee, by faith, the meteor legate of free thought, linger over the manger of Bethlehem; the vail is rent ; it ſhoots from Calvary in its path of empire.

By faith, it ſpans the firmament with the arc of promiſe, to its watch and ward, a fixed ſtar, over the cradle of human rights.

Oppreſſed of all lands, you are pilgrims to its ſhrine, and Herod alſo has come to worſhip ; will you be apoſtles of that holy ſymbol or puppets of a blind creed ?

You are moulding the fate of diſtant ages ; as the ſtern minutes are chaſing the ſhadows of time, invoke, not your ſaints, but the nobler inſtincts God has breathed into your hearts ; go, not to the Bulls of your Leos and Borgias ; go, kneel and watch at Gethſemane ; go, aſk the oracle of Olivet, if the faith that forgot her maſk in the bloody revels of Bartholomew's night, till every Catholic heart had beat *Amen* to the *Gloria in Excelſis* of the Vatican —if the faith that left her maſk at the farce of Trent with the ſhout that ſhook the dome, CURSED, CURSED, CURSED BE ALL HERETICS—ſhall be the faith of your children ?

We have freely taſked the magnanimity of ſtrength, to tone the ungracioufneſs of truth, almoſt at her peril ; gladly, with the ſanction of duty, would we walk backward with our ſiſter's garments and cover our ſiſter's ſhame.

New York.

Preface

RIVATE judgment, the giſt of the Reforma-
tion, is denounced by the Church of Rome, as
the ſource of error and ſchiſm : the highway of
atheiſm and hereſy.

In the blindneſs of zeal, ſhe forgets that conviction relates
to faith, as the ſolar rays to viſion, or as digeſtion to aſſimi-
lation.

Boſſuet's raid on Proteſtant variances, the eloquent eſſays
of Bellarmin, Duperron and Baronius all challenge our
reaſon.   Is Rome the rule of faith, the touchſtone of truth,
becauſe ſhe claims the proxy of omnipotence?   does ſhe
aſſume the baton of infallibility?   we examine her creden-

tials; we collate the Fathers with the decretals and councils.

If ſhe exults in unity: to find that one true united Church; we ſcan her records, which rebuke her idle boaſt with the quarrels of Janſeniſts, of Moliniſts, of Quietiſts, of the Church of Abbé Châtel, of Ultramontaniſts, and of Gallicans with their endleſs conteſts.

To unravel her ſucceſſion: we trace her bickerings through centuries, and encounter a dilemma, too ſubtle for the Council of Conſtance, which *votes itſelf above the Papacy and depoſes in a breath three ſovereign Pontiffs.*[1]

Should a Proteſtant, Jew or Heathen ſeek ghoſtly counſel, a prieſt will arrogate the courſe he denies to them; whenever Rome warns us, that there is no ſafety beyond her pale, ſhe exhorts with Paul; *prove all things, hold faſt that which is good.*

If reſearch is deluſive, if truth may be ſought only in the ruts of authority: our miſſions are vicious: all ſhould

---

[1] This ſchiſm began in 1378: was ſuſpended in 1414 by the Council of Conſtance, and forthwith renewed; ſurvived to the Council of Bâle in 1431, and ended in 1477 by the abdication of Felix V. who conſented to reſume his cardinalate, though elected Pope by the Council of Bâle.

cling to the faith of their Fathers: there live, and there die.

Iſlam has her vouchers: ſhe dooms the pervert to death, and threatens him with the pains and gates of hell.

Let us imagine a colliſion between Turks and Pápiſts.

The *locum tenens* of God cannot err in faith: the language of our Doctors rejoins the Moſlem.

The Popes have an unbroken ſucceſſion: ſo alſo have our Imams: and Caliphs *ſuperadd temporal to ſpiritual power.*

Rome may glory in the pomp of her temples, in her ſolemn ritual, in her diſcipline, in her faſts: Iſlam alſo has her ſtately moſques, preſcribed prayers, and her vigils, more rigid than thoſe of Rome.

Does Rome ban with hereſy all who reject her rule? the diſciples of Ali and Omar mutually curſe: they have their ſaints, pilgrims and legends: 'tis true, they lack a holy office, armed with the terrors of the ſtake and rack to awe the froward, and win ſheep to the Prophet's fold: but in con-queſt, heretics muſt elect between the Koran and the bow-ſtring.

Or ſuppoſe an infidel, convinced of inſpired truth, and the

completion of prophefy, perplexed by jarring creeds : you quote your councils, your divines, your decrees of fucceffion.

He learns that the Greek Church, the Arminian, Nefto-rian, Ethiopian has each her divines, her councils and her fucceffion : he fifts their ftandards ; how can he elfe decide between a breaker and worfhipper of images, who both appeal to Ecumenical Councils ?

The cyclic logic, " Rome has Scripture authority, and Rome is the exponent of Scripture," ignores the wholefome checks of judge and party.

To enfure our obedience, a Church muft hold God's warrant : his word is our ftay and ftaff : *fearch the Scriptures, for in them ye think ye have eternal life, and they are they which teftify of me : Believe not every Spirit, but try the Spirits, whether they are of God : bleffed is he that readeth, and they that hear the words of this prophefy.*

The youth of Timothy was devoted to facred ftudy, and the Bereans were applauded *for fearching the Scriptures daily, whether thofe things were fo.*

Cheered by Chrift's promife of his Holy Spirit to guide him into all truth, the Chriftian bears in mind, that *the*

Heavens and the Earth ſhall paſs away, but the words of Chriſt paſs not away; that all Scripture is given by inſpiration of God, and is profitable for doƐrine, for reproof, for correƐion, for inſtruƐiㅁ in righteouſneſs.

Submiſſion to God's word is the Shibboleth of the Reformation : the Socinian, with whom the Romaniſts wiſh to confound us,—neither Chriſtian nor infidel—exalts reaſon above the Bible, and with the daring of criticiſm, rejeƐs any faƐ, or any doƐrine, that humbles his pride or paſſes his wiſdom.

Although the Scriptures may often aſſert, yet I do not believe that Chriſt is God : for I hold it to be abſurd to believe that which is beyond the reach of my reaſon : is the language of Smalcius, their leading polemic.

The Bible, ſays Prieſtly, chief of a kindred ſchool : *was written with no particular inſpiration.*[1]

Such, are not the views of the Reformation : the word of God is our ſole guide, our light and hope : crying with Samuel ; *ſpeak, Lord, for thy ſervants hear.*

---

[1] Prieſtly—Hiſtoire des opinions primitives, vol. 4. p. 5. Belſham ſur Wilberforce, p. 19. Inveſtigations calmes—pp. 451, 452.

Variance gives bolder relief to the unity of our faith : hallelujahs rife above the din of difcord : Anglican and Gallican : Helvetian and Lutheran ; all profefs the fall of man ; the incarnate word ; falvation through the Atonement ; a trinity in unity : *knowing nothing fave Jefus Chrift,* and the affluence of his grace and love.

Rome confines her Laity to her dicta, left the ftudy of Scripture might wreck them on the Scylla or Charybdis of herefy or infidelity.

Experience fhows, how ill-fuftained are they in the hour of death, who rely on human faith : the Prieft pronounces the words of abfolution : the confcience anfwers ; *there is no peace.*

We humbly confide the weal of Chrift's Church, to the broadcaft of his Holy word : that man may quench his thirft at the fountain of living waters.

God grant that thefe letters may refcue many *from Babylon, that they receive not of her plagues.*

Letter First.

Sir,

 Y the teſt I gave you when we laſt met, it is
eaſy to determine, if the Fathers allowed the
ſubſtantial preſence of Chriſt's body and blood
in the Euchariſt : their views are ſubordinate only to Scripture, with which we now confront the Roman dogma.

Two points compriſe the iſſue.

Is the Bible our rule of faith ?

What are its teachings ?

You, a Chriſtian by grace, will not queſtion, if Holy Writ
announces to man the whole counſel of God, and invokes in
behalf of ſaving truths, even the aid of example and precept.
You will admit, that its inſpired penmen would not ignore a

grave myſtery; a covenant of mercy, involving faith and practice, and that all Revelation muſt harmonize.

Liſten with candor to the leſſons of inſpiration : I engage, to tear the maſk of Divine authority from this monkiſh fiction.

We fault the Church of Rome with

𝕿𝖍𝖊 𝖔𝖗𝖆𝖑 𝖒𝖆𝖓𝖉𝖚𝖈𝖆𝖙𝖎𝖔𝖓 𝖔𝖋 𝖙𝖍𝖊 𝕷𝖔𝖗𝖉'𝖘 𝖇𝖔𝖉𝖞 ;

𝕿𝖍𝖊 𝖒𝖆𝖙𝖊𝖗𝖎𝖆𝖑 𝖕𝖗𝖊𝖋𝖊𝖓𝖈𝖊 ;

𝕿𝖍𝖊 𝖈𝖍𝖆𝖓𝖌𝖊 𝖔𝖋 𝖋𝖚𝖇𝖋𝖙𝖆𝖓𝖈𝖊 ;

𝕿𝖍𝖊 𝖜𝖔𝖗𝖋𝖍𝖎𝖕 𝖔𝖋 𝖙𝖍𝖊 𝕾𝖆𝖈𝖗𝖆𝖒𝖊𝖓𝖙 ;

𝖂𝖎𝖙𝖍𝖍𝖔𝖑𝖉𝖎𝖓𝖌 𝖙𝖍𝖊 𝕮𝖚𝖕 ; and

𝕿𝖍𝖊 𝖋𝖆𝖈𝖗𝖎𝖋𝖎𝖈𝖊 𝖔𝖋 𝖙𝖍𝖊 𝖒𝖆𝖋𝖘.

This Church aſſumes a literal eating from the words of the inſtitution and the ſixth chapter of St. John : we rely on Origen and Auguſtine, thoſe great lights of the primitive Church, and on Jeſus Chriſt, as ſafe teachers of divine truth.

If we render literally thoſe words of Jeſus Chriſt : if you do not eat my fleſh and drink my blood : that letter kills,[1] is the emphatic dictum of Origen.

---

[1] Homil. vii. in Leviticum.

Auguſtine ſuſtains him ; *the language that prohibits a wrong, or commands ſomething uſeful or beneficent is not figurative : but if it commands a crime, or forbids what is beneficent or uſeful, it is metaphorical, hence the mandate ; to eat the fleſh of the ſon of man, and drink his blood; enjoins a communion with his paſſion, in recalling profitably and ſweetly that his fleſh was torn for our ſins.*[1]

Our Lord, as if to foreſtall all poſſible cavil, promptly defines his ordinance : *the words that I ſpeak unto you, they are ſpirit, and they are life :*[2] and as Rome admits, that, Chriſt here directs a ſpiritual and quickening conſtruction of his language, ſuch ſenſe muſt warrant a ſtrict eating, or fails to juſtify her theory.

This *United* Church writhing under his laſh, charges Origen with myſtic tendencies ; and we reply ; could that great divine, believing that he actually ſwallowed the fleſh and blood of his Redeemer, aſſert, *that the letter kills* and eſcape conviction of falſchood and blaſphemy? She con-

[1] Auguſt. Lib. iii. cap. xvi. de doctrina chriſtiana.
[2] John vi. 53, 63.

E

tends, that Auguſtine in the above citation conformed to the ruling of Rome, rejecting only, the ſenſe of the Caper- naites; a ſtrange deluſion indeed, as he clings to the metaphor, leſt the letter might command a wrong or a crime.

Let us humor for a moment the caprice of our literal friends.

With touching modeſty, and in deference to revelation, they exclude our ſenſes—as falſe witneſſes in matters of faith :—we renounce our ſenſes—are they now content?— far from it—with ſtill more engaging *naïveté*, they demand the ſurrender of our reaſon—as a ſacrifice to God—and we ſubmit, if God requires it.

But what is this long expected Revelation, this full equivalent to all the functions of body and ſoul, and every inſtinct of nature? a ſingle phraſe—by the Son of God, Origen and Auguſtine pronounced allegorical, by Rome, literal : has fatuity a lower deep?

To identify the language of John with that of Chriſt, you will pleaſe obſerve that the words : *take, eat, this is my body ;* and, *he that does not eat my fleſh and drink my blood,* though not ſpoken in connection, are but varied terms : and

that as both, if either, are bound by a quickening and
fpiritual fenfe, the letter of both, if either, *muſt ſeem to command a crime.*

I now challenge a denial of any of theſe points.

If the oral, has ſcripture authority, it is confined to the
above and parallel texts.

Thoſe paſſages ſhould receive a figurative, ſpiritual, and
quickening ſenſe on the authority of Origen, Auguſtine and
of Chriſt himſelf.

That in ſuch terms, we are not bound to ſeek a groſs eating.

I further inſiſt, that if the letter is vague and inconſiſtent,
or falſe and deluſive, we are limited to the figure.

Our Lord was wont to illuſtrate his leſſons : he talks with
fiſhermen ; the preaching of the Goſpel is imaged by a
myſtical fiſhing : near a fountain—water, is the emblem of
his grace—he preſſes the figure ; water, as guſhing up into
endleſs life ; whoſo drinks thereof ſhall never thirſt.

To Nicodemus, he ſays : *except a man be born again, he
cannot ſee the kingdom of God,*[1] and who ſo ſimple as Nicode-

---

[1] John iii. 3.

mus, and aſks : how can a man re-enter his mother's womb ?

To the hungry throng : *labor not for the meat which periſheth, but for that meat which endureth to everlaſting life :*[1] *that it is his meat to do the will of his father.*

Before ſpeaking of eating his fleſh, and drinking his blood : he declares—*that he is the living bread, which came down from heaven and whoſoever ſhall eat thereof ſhall never hunger,*[2] and all admit the bread to be an image, and the hunger ſpiritual.

Again, he ſays, *he that eateth my fleſh and drinketh my blood, dwelleth in me,*[3] and no one imagines that we can dwell in Chriſt in a proper ſenſe : he then repeats : *this is that bread which came down from Heaven, he that eateth of this bread ſhall live for ever.*[4]

The Papal Church here makes a merit of neceſſity, as Chriſt cannot be properly bread, nor bread properly Chriſt, and limits her letter to the terms *eating* and *drinking.*

---

[1] John vi. 27.   [2] John vi. 35, 50, 51.
[3] John vi. 56.   [4] John vi. 58.

There then is the proper *sense*, *swarming* with figures; the letter, engulfed in metaphor.

Jesus was rebuking the multitude which had *said : that Moses had given their fathers bread from heaven : but what sign shewest thou then, that we may see, and believe thee?*[1]

He shews his gift to be greater than that of *Moses* : the promised bread, is *living ;* the true bread of Heaven ; he contrasts it with the manna.

He then calls that living bread himself ; his flesh ; and thus exalts the living bread over the manna : they who eat the manna would hunger again, while whoever eat this bread would hunger no more ; they who eat the manna died, but whoso eat this bread would live for ever.

Such are the teachings of *Jesus* Christ, repeated and enforced by his own lips ; and in *such sense*, he requires us to feed on his flesh and blood.

Now, may I ask our opponents when citing John's Gospel ; either, to deny that *such* are the *lessons* of Christ, or being *such* they favor an oral eating.

---

[1] John vi. 30, 31.

It seems to me, that Chrift here oppofes the carnal to the spiritual; the manna, a fenfual bread to his flefh an emblem of bread: the effect of the manna, a mortal life, to the efficacy of his flefh, eternal life : the manna feeds the body, his flefh feeds the heart : thus far no Chriftian can diffent.

If then, the flefh of Chrift be but the type of bread, meet only to cherifh the foul and animate the fpirit; does a ftrict confumption of his flefh, or the nourifhment of our fouls by a fymbolic bread, anfwer to an eating in fpirit and in faith?

Now, if Chrift, in figure, promifes bread from Heaven in contraft to the manna—in figure, declares his flefh to be that bread—in figure, affirms its fufficiency to fatisfy for ever, and its all fufficiency for falvation : I infift, that an exprefs apo-calypfe only can clothe the words *eating* and *drinking* with a proper and literal fenfe.

We are told, that in the phrafe : *he who eats the bread that I fhall give him, fhall never hunger :* though the bread is an image, and the hunger ideal : the *eating*, muft be literal to efcape the ban of herefy.

In our view, the ideas of hunger, bread, and eating feem to bear fuch clofe and mutual relation, that when found united, and dependent, it is natural to refer them all, either to the letter or the metaphor.

And when our Lord fubjoins, *except ye eat the flefh of the Son of Man*,[1] he implies the flefh which he calls bread : a bread capable of fatisfying.

This is no illufion of fancy, it is the emphatic language of our Lord : *the bread that I will give is my flefh*.[2]

With what confcience can they claim, that a flefh which they admit to be mere bread, and can fatisfy, but in figure, fhould be eaten properly ?

I alfo contend, that the letter mars, while the trope retains the truth and force of Chrift's teachings.

The eating in St. John has two falient traits.

It is a condition of falvation : *verily I fay unto you ; except ye eat the flefh of the Son of Man, and drink his blood, ye have no life in you :*[3] It is all fufficient : *whofo eateth my flefh and drinketh my blood, hath eternal life, and I will raife him up at the laft day.*[4]

---

[1] John vi. 53.   [2] John vi. 51.
[3] John vi. 53.   [4] John vi. 54.

Nor do I stand on debateable ground in alleging, that there is a spiritual eating of Christ's body by faith.

The oral eating, is not essential, as the converted thief, the catechumen or newly baptised, barred by death or just hindrance from taking Christ in his stomach, does not forfeit grace.

It is not conclusive, as the standards of Rome denounce the mockery of an eating, without the concurrence of the heart ; whereas the spiritual eating, is both a rule of faith, and all sufficient, the true partaker in act, or will having already passed from death to life.

Is then the carnal, void of every feature required by John's Gospel, or the spiritual eating which embraces all those features, to be learned from the lessons of Christ ?

The Latin Church now seeks to evade the issue by garbling Christ's ordinance, she limits his promises to worthy eaters of his flesh.

Before adopting this view, I demand its authority : reliance on St. Paul is hopeless : he applies the terms, worthy and unworthy, only to the reception of the bread : whoso eateth the flesh of Christ, eats it worthily ; because it is eaten in spirit and in faith.

Judas ate the bread of our Saviour, ſays Auguſtine, but he did not eat the bread, which is the Saviour, being an unworthy recipient.

However that may be, can we reconcile this reſtriction with the tenor of Chriſt's preaching to the Jews? that his fleſh, not the manna, is the true celeſtial bread ; as the manna could not ſave their fathers from death ; but, his fleſh ſecures eternal life to thoſe who eat it.

He ſimply compares the eating of his fleſh, with the eating of the manna, irreſpective of perſonal merit.

Mark, Sir, how it enervates his language ; who can doubt, if the fleſh of Jeſus Chriſt, rent for our ſins, the object of our faith and truſt, is more precious to us, than was the manna to the Iſraelites? but why ſhould the ſtrict eating of that fleſh, by the faithful or faithleſs, have more efficacy than the bread of Moſes?

The manna could not ſave the Jews from temporal or eternal death, ſo, the groſs reception of Chriſt's fleſh, exempts men, neither from the death of the body, as they remain mortal ; nor from the death of the ſoul, as they are ſinners ſtill : by faith only are we ſaved.

If then, a feeding on Chriſt by faith has all the poſſible efficacy of the manna, and its actual deglutition has no more efficacy than the manna : the ſpiritual, not the oral, ſuſtains the truth and force of his teachings.

Do we live and dwell in Chriſt, by his entrance into our throats, or into our hearts? by taking his fleſh into our mouths, or through the exerciſe of faith in the merits of that fleſh, mangled for our ſins?

Would not a Chriſtian in a Pagan land, without acceſs to the holy table lead a ſpiritual life? Will not Rome allow that after the bread and wine have paſſed from the viſcera in the courſe of nature, the elements of life remain in the heart? Are not faith and repentance the conſtituents of ſpiritual life? how then can that eating be ſenſual, which in contraſt to the manna, is lifegiving; life to the ſoul; life eternal?

Other paſſages in John fortify our caſe : *I am the bread of life ; he that cometh to me, ſhall never hunger ; and he that believeth on me ſhall never thirſt.*[1]

---

[1] John vi. 35.

The claufes; *he that cometh to me,* and *he that eateth my flefh: he that believeth on me,* and, *he that drinketh my blood,* are obvious equipollents in the diction of our Lord.

In the fame chapter, we alfo read, of a lifegiving eating; the neglect of which is death: this eating, muft be oral folely, or folely fpiritual, or fpiritual and oral; in which laft fenfe, whofo eateth not Chrift's flefh, and drinketh not his blood, both by mouth and faith, hath no life in him.

Our Lord did not command the oral folely, as the unholy derive no benefit therefrom : nor the joint reception, as many can commune only in the defire of the heart: ergo: thofe texts enjoin a fpiritual eating of his body.

Again, Sir, Scripture is either metaphorical, or literal : if thofe words in John are figurative, Rome admits a fymbolic eating; if literal, confiftency demands a proper drinking of the blood.

A natural drinking differs from a natural eating, unlefs eating and drinking are fynonyms : now the blood of Chrift, by the ufage of Rome, is no more drunk than eaten, nor eaten than drunk; as the blood, not parted from his veins is received in the guife of bread and wine.

There being no mean between real and typical *ſleep*, we are bound to believe that the diſciples knew no mean, between drinking Chriſt's blood figuratively, and literally.

Thoſe ſimple, earneſt men, unſchooled in metaphyſics, who had never read Aquinas nor Scotus, would have inferred, that their maſter ſpoke of drinking his blood either ſpiritually or carnally : *dwell in me : I am the vine; I am the way; I am the door; I am the bread of life ; whoſoever believeth in me, out of his belly ſhall flow rivers of living waters;* with like tropes ringing in their ears, and training their minds to recognize in figures, the veiling of ſpiritual precepts under ſenſible images.

We now ſubmit, that we are not chargeable with verbal criticiſm and wild theory in affirming, that Chriſt's literal preſcript, *to drink his blood*, implies a literal drinking

That the reception of Chriſt's body, with blood in his veins, under the forms of bread and wine, being no leſs an eating than a drinking, is not a proper drinking of his blood.

That, as an injunction to eat his fleſh, and drink his blood, literally, cannot be obeyed in the Supper, nor elſewhere, we are confined to the metaphor.

Verily, Sir, that is a falfe pofition, which rejeĉts the figure, but dares not claim the letter: which culls from an allegorical chapter, two lone phrafes, for which they exaĉt a rigid fenfe, yet curfes thofe who do not drink our Lord's blood in a manner, not happily defined, but neither typical nor proper.

Carelefs, if the language of the Son of God is incoherent, unconcerned, if its beauty, truth, and power are marred; the abortive letter muft refute itfelf.

At war with Scripture, with fenfe, and with reafon, we leave them at variance with themfelves: fo much for the fixth chapter of John.

I am, &c, &c.

Letter Second.

S we approach the words of the ordinance,[1] call to mind that St. Paul conſtantly ſtyles the Eu-chariſt, Bread:[2] that the diſciples continued ſteadfaſtly in prayer and in breaking of bread:[3] that Jeſus Chriſt vaniſhed from their ſight, after breaking bread:[4] all which, and like paſſages are allowed alluſions to actual Sacraments.

Were Paul and Luke at variance with Chriſt, we ſhould be bound by the higher law, but as they ſpake with his Spirit, we muſt ſeek to harmonize their teachings.

The Church of Rome contends, that Paul applies the

---

[1] Matt. xxvi. 26.   Mark xiv. 22.   Luke xxii. 19.
[2] 1 Cor. xi. 23, 24, 25, &c.   [3] Acts ii. 42.   [4] Luke xxiv. 30, 31.

term bread to the body of Chriſt, becauſe his body is veiled under the accidents of bread: we hold, that our Lord honored the bread with the name of his body, in view, only, of that body's myſtic preſence: hence, our iſſue with Rome, is not, whether Scripture refers in figure to the Euchariſt; but whether, it employs the figure, in calling the Euchariſt, the body of Chriſt.

I claim that we are free to conſult:

𝔒𝔲𝔯 ſ𝔢𝔫ſ𝔢𝔰:

𝔒𝔲𝔯 𝔯𝔢𝔞ſ𝔬𝔫:

𝔗𝔥𝔢 𝔥𝔬𝔩𝔶 𝔖𝔠𝔯𝔦𝔭𝔱𝔲𝔯𝔢𝔰:

And 𝔱𝔥𝔢 𝔞𝔫𝔞𝔩𝔬𝔤𝔶 𝔬𝔣 𝔣𝔞𝔦𝔱𝔥.

Senſe. We rely on the ſenſes, becauſe the Son of God calls them as witneſſes to his reſurrection, ſaying to his diſ-ciples, *Handle me and ſee,*[1] and who will doubt, that the proof tendered by Chriſt, as a voucher for his truth, is com-petent to decide the ſpirit of his language?

The ſenſes aver that the Euchariſt is bread, and that Chriſt ſpeaks in figure, not Paul and Luke.

---

[1] Luke xxiv. 39.

Senſes and Reaſon.

Reaſon aſſures us, that as the ſimple body of Chriſt cannot be in each atom of the bread, in full volume, and proportion : a ſynchronous tenant of divers places, it is more rational to adopt the clearer phraſe of St. Paul than the obſcurer term employed by our Lord.

The rejection of reaſon as witneſs againſt faith, aſſumes the ſtandards of Rome to be the arbiter of Chriſt's language : when ſhe ſhews her doctrine to be the doctrine of inſpiration, I ſilence my reaſon ; until then, ſhe muſt not forbid me its aid, when perplexed between the leſſons of Chriſt and his apoſtles.

And who are they that ſcorn the evidence of reaſon and ſenſe ? even they, whoſe ſenſes reveal the exiſtence of the bread, and whoſe reaſon confirms their faith in Chriſt's ſacramental preſence ; which if unſeen, muſt be in the nature of ſpirit, unleſs ſenſe and reaſon, like the cloud-guide of Iſrael, are light to them, but darkneſs to us.

The Latin theory would be more plauſible, were we arrayed againſt the ſacred Canon—liſten—*Jeſus Chriſt is gone—he has left the earth—we ſhall have him no more with us—we muſt raiſe our hearts on high, where Jeſus is ſeated at*

*the right hand of God the Father—if he were on earth, he
would not even be Prieſt—we muſt wait until he ſhall come as
the lightning, which ſhineth from the Eaſt even unto the Weſt ;
and the Heavens ſhall be his habitation until the re-eſtabliſh-
ment of all things.*

Such is the tenor of Scripture, which never alludes to preſence viſible, natural nor latent.

Scripture. This tenet jars with ſacred hiſtory : our Lord,
before quitting the earth, often declares *that he leaves the
Earth and goes to the Father.*

The Church of Rome, here, draws her lines of viſible, and
inviſible preſence, forgetting, that if Chriſt intended, that his
cloaked humanity ſhould dwell on the earth, and enter the
mouths and ſtomachs of his diſciples, he would ſurely have
noticed ſo conſoling a faƈt, when in the ſadneſs of their
hearts, he calls them his friends ; his little children ; aſſures
them tenderly of his love, and promiſes *not to leave them com-
fortleſs ; and that he would ſend a Comforter who would guide
them into all truth.*

The Son of God bars all preſence, warranting outlay in
behalf of his humanity : *for ye have the poor with you always,*

and whenfoever ye will, ye may do them good, but me, ye have not always.[1]

He here excludes, not merely that phyfical prefence, admitting alms or expenfe, like Mary's honorary unction, whofe value, provoked the cenfure of Judas; but, alfo, that occult prefence, which prompts the coftly pageants of Rome.

Analogy. Perhaps, the letter may elicit light from the harmony of infpired truth.

The affumption of the flefh is a folemn myftery, paffing human reafon; a mean of man's falvation, and of God's glory.

This Roman dogma trenches on the laws of nature, expofes the Meffiah to ufelefs fhame and countlefs hazards in the facrificial hands of a thoufand priefts.

The Bible teaches no more plainly that Redemption is the object of the Incarnation, than that the Euchariſt is a token of Chriſt's death : *this do ye, for as often as ye eat this bread, &c, ye do fhew the Lord's death till he come.*[2]

It is clear, that the Incarnation muſt precede Redemption,

---

[1] John xii. 8.   Mark xiv. 7.   [2] 1 Cor. xi. 26.

as the atonement is a decree of God, and a demand of the law : but it is not clear, that Chriſt's natural fleſh and blood ſhould be ſwallowed by us, in memory of his death ; while a type, conſecrated with the name of his body, as a fixed ſymbol of that body broken for us, ſatisfies his manifeſt purpoſe.

Rome urges the letter of a ſingle paſſage ; we produce many, with like claims—we conflict—the ſenſes, reaſon, Scripture and analogy ſuſtain us and condemn her.

If you bear in mind that Paul is the exponent of Chriſt, not Chriſt of Paul, and that ſcholia are more literal than the text, I will not fear your verdict.

I now offer, to abandon the iſſue, or prove the words of Paul to be ſuſceptive only of the letter, and thoſe of Chriſt, only of the figure.

We will ſift the deſign of St. Paul, in the eleventh chapter of the firſt Corinthians.

It is well known, that the early Chriſtians held their agapæ after public worſhip, which love feaſts cloſed with the communion ; and that the Corinthians at ſuch times, were prone to exceſs.

Now let Paul ſpeak—*When ye come together into one*

place, this is not to eat the Lord's supper. ' For in eating, every one taketh before other his own supper; and one is hungry and another is drunken. What! have ye not houses to eat and to drink in? or despise ye the Church of God, and shame them that have not? What shall I say to you? Shall I praise you in this? I praise you not.

For I have received of the Lord, that which I delivered unto you, that the Lord Jesus, the same night in which he was betrayed, took bread: and when he had given thanks, he brake it, and said, take, eat: this is my body, which is broken for you: this do in remembrance of me. After the same manner, he also took the cup, when he had supped, saying, this cup is the New Testament in my blood: this do ye, as oft as ye drink it, in remembrance of me.

For as often as ye eat this bread, and drink this cup, ye do shew the Lord's death till he come.

Wherefore, whosoever shall eat this bread, and drink this cup of the Lord, unworthily, shall be guilty of the body and blood of the Lord.

But let a man examine himself, and so let him eat of that bread and drink of that cup.

For he that eateth and drinketh unworthily, eateth and drinketh damnation to himfelf, not difcerning the Lord's body.

This extract, in extenfo ; a variance from the ufage of Rome, which adroitly culls the text, in defiance of the context, is due to the argument.

It is obvious that the Corinthians ate the bread with a licenfe, that provoked the reproof of the apoftle, who preffed the fanctity of the fupper.

With thefe fimple truths, we thwart the ruling of Rome, and prove our view to be juft and natural.

The apoftle charges them with greedinefs and drunkennefs, *they do not eat the fupper of the Lord, they defpife the Church of God: he had not inftituted the Eucharift, but was commanded by his Mafter to celebrate it.*

Paul fhews that the ordinance was defigned, to recall Chrift's death, and thus points a climax: *he who eats or drinks unworthily, eats and drinks damnation to himfelf.*

Is it debateable, if thofe pledges and fymbols which our Lord ordained and hallowed with the name of his body and blood, are defiled by irreverence ?

Imagine, St. Paul, in communion with the Vatican, and

his hearers guilty of taking Chriſt's fleſh and blood into ſtomachs gorged with meat and wine.

In what ſcathing terms would he brand ſuch mockery of the elements; in what tones of thunder, would he hurl the curſe of Rome at ſuch loathſome ſacrilege?

Liſten—*The Corinthians deſpiſe the Church of God*: ſcorching rebuke, forſooth, to men who ſtain the maſs with the revels of the Bacchanal : *its objeƐ is to revive in memory the death of Chriſt till he come*, a gentle demur, to the pollution of their Saviour's real fleſh and blood.

But hark ; the apoſtle reſerves his cenſure?

No ſir; he then terms the Euchariſt bread, in three diſtinƐ paſſages : for, as often as ye eat this bread, and drink this cup, ye do ſhew, &c. Wherefore, whoſoever ſhall eat this bread, and drink this cup of the Lord, ſhall be guilty, &c. let each one examine himſelf, and ſo let him eat of that bread, &c.

Then, if ever, would and ſhould he have urged the ſignificance and dignity of that holy myſtery, and clothed it with awe : but mark; he calls it bread, not the body of the Lord; why ſo lukewarm? Marvellous indeed, if Paul was Papiſtic.

Chemical Change in the Eucharift.

Shall I yield even this point? is fo much deference due to our biaffed friends? be it fo—all is erafed.

I now fcale their ramparts, and difmifs all I have faid, unlefs I prove :—

𝕿𝖍𝖆𝖙 𝖙𝖍𝖊 𝖙𝖗𝖔𝖕𝖊 𝖎𝖘 𝖓𝖊𝖎𝖙𝖍𝖊𝖗 𝖘𝖙𝖗𝖆𝖓𝖌𝖊 𝖓𝖔𝖗 𝖘𝖙𝖗𝖆𝖎𝖓𝖊𝖉 :

𝕴𝖙 𝖍𝖆𝖉 𝖆 𝖘𝖎𝖌𝖓𝖆𝖑 𝖋𝖎𝖙𝖓𝖊𝖘𝖘 :

𝕿𝖍𝖊 𝖉𝖎𝖘𝖈𝖎𝖕𝖑𝖊𝖘 𝖆𝖉𝖔𝖕𝖙𝖊𝖉 𝖎𝖙 :

𝕽𝖔𝖒𝖊 𝖈𝖆𝖓𝖓𝖔𝖙 𝖊𝖘𝖈𝖆𝖕𝖊 𝖎𝖙 :

𝕿𝖍𝖊 𝖑𝖊𝖙𝖙𝖊𝖗 𝖎𝖘 𝖋𝖔𝖗𝖈𝖊𝖉 𝖆𝖓𝖉 𝖆𝖇𝖘𝖚𝖗𝖉 :

Firft—Imagery was habitual to our Lord; to Peter, he fays; *if I wafh thee not, thou haft no part with me :*[1] hear him, in the agony of the crofs, confiding the bleffed virgin to St. John—*woman, behold thy fon ; then faith he to the difciple— behold thy mother.*[2]

Are Sacraments excepted? the Pafchal Lamb a mere token of the angel's paffing over the houfes of Ifrael, was ftyled the Paffover or Paffage : does the prefcript of a Rite call for proper terms? No Sir, I hold that the Saviour in ordaining the bread and wine, figns of his bruifed body, and fpilled

---

[1] John xiii. 8.   [2] John xix. 26, 27.

blood, fhould have challenged reverence for the fymbols, by hallowing them with the names of the things fignified.

In the new covenant, Baptifm is the wafhing of Regeneration, and in the language of Paul, *we are buried with Jefus Chrift by baptifm unto death.*[1]

Thus, in every afpect, be it fpeaker, or hearer, fubject or incidents, there is no ftrain in the figure.

Second. The occafion fuggefted the metaphor. It is familiar hiftory, that the epoch of the advent was prone to allegory, and myftery : the day, as well as the Lamb bore the name of the Angel's paffage.

A cuftom, however, at the fupper of the Paffover, is emphatic : the father of the family took a piece of bread, and ate it with bitter herbs : reciting the formula—*This is the bread of mifery and affliction, that our fathers ate in Egypt : let him that is an hungered come and eat ;* a form furely not adopted by the Jews from courtefy to us, but derived from the fixteenth chapter of Deuteronomy ; *feven days fhalt thou eat unleavened bread therewith, even the bread of affliction.*

[1] Romans vi. 4.

H

Moderate wit may here difcern the exemplar of the Sacrament : our Lord chofe the immerfion of Jewifh Neophytes as a model for Baptifm; in like manner, he adapted a Jewifh rite to the Eucharift.

As the bread, fteeped in bitter fauce, ferved to recall the affliction of their fathers; fo, would the broken bread be an emblem of Chrift's body, bruifed on the crofs.

Thus runs the ritual of the Paffover : *this is the bread of mifery and affliction, which our fathers ate in Egypt : let him that is an hungered come and eat.*

Take, eat, this is my body, broken for you, is the language of the laft fupper : their affinity is obvious.

We paufe, to meet the plea that the difciples who had not yet regarded the bread, as a type, would have found equal obfcurity in the phrafes: *this is my body: this tree is Alexander.*

Strange as it may feem, this forry conceit brandifhed in triumph twenty-five times in two hundred pages, is the gift of M. Arnauld's pofition : his armor offenfive and defenfive.

It is untrue, that our Lord always announced a metaphor.

To Nicodemus, who had faid, *Rabbi, we know that thou art a teacher come from God, for no man can do thofe miracles that thou doeft, except God be with him:* Jefus anfwers, *verily; verily; I fay unto thee; except a man be born again he cannot fee the Kingdom of God.*[1]

The notion of Nicodemus was coarfe and literal; the figure was patent from the conflict of the letter, as the phrafe : *this that I have taken is my body broken for you,* was due caution to the difciples.

If you call to mind, that notice with, or following a metaphor, derives force from tranfient doubt, the fophifm is patent.

If talking with a friend of the battles of Alexander, I fay, pointing to a tree; *That tree is Alexander,* however low he may rate my judgment, he will not imagine that I miftake a plant for the victor at Arbela; but when I add, *fancy his army here; the Perfian there;* his fufpenfe ceafes.

I further fay that even without notice, the idea of an

---

[1] John iii. 2, 3.

objeĉt in the hand of Chriſt, being the body of Chriſt, condemns the letter.

The mental ſhock would ſurely have ſecured an inſtant's pauſe, until hearing their maſter inſtitute a memorial of his death, the diſciples could not doubt his meaning; *this will repreſent to you my broken body till I come;* irreſpeĉtive even, of the equivalence of the verbs *is* and *ſignify* in the language in which they were ſpoken.

We thank the Author for raiſing the queſtion of probability.

Were the diſciples ready to rejeĉt their ſenſes, till then never doubted; thoſe ſenſes, which had witneſſed the miracles of our Lord; thoſe channels of every truth that underlies our faith?

Were they free to concede, that a body can at once, fill divers places, and that they took their maſter's body from their maſter's hand, in ſpite of their life tried reaſon?

Had they leiſure to ponder on effeĉts without cauſe, or on the import of the verb *is* (in the Syrian dialeĉt of the period, I repeat, a term convertible with *ſignify*,)[1] had they the

---

[1] Hebræo Aramæan.

acutenefs at fuch a time, to difcern Chrift's body in the bread, and a change initial and in abeyance till the words of confecration were fully uttered?

Subtlety, fharpened by centuries of wrangling, may difcover that Chrift did not intend the bread, when he faid ; giving, what he had taken, and broken ; *this is*, or, if the pronoun applies to the bread, that the bread is his actual body ; but men, who in their fimplicity would queftion, one with another ; *what the rifing of the dead fhould mean?* could fcarcely be equal to fuch fcholaftic nicety.

Prefumption favors us ; The myfteries of the day ; the bread of mifery and affliction ; fenfe, reafon ; the dimnefs of the letter ; the difciples' artleffnefs ; the act of Chrift who took, brake and gave the bread ; its prompt expofition in thofe pregnant words ; *do this in remembrance of me;* his habitual imagery, were each, full notice of the figure ; and I marvel much, that fo adroit a difputant, in framing laws of language for us, referves none for himfelf.

Third. You may arrive at the impreffions of the difciples, by noting the abfence of any act of worfhip ; there was no clamor for the folution of a myftery ; not even a change of posture; so palpable was the figure, not a question was asked; not a comment made; not a word spoken.

Was this apathy the fruit of private teachings? their master had foretold his rising from the grave: strange indeed, that after waiving their sight, and all their senses to assume his entrance into their stomachs, they would not trust their eyes in proof of his resurrection; supposing it a dream.

Could those men, on the warrant of a few words, and in defiance of their senses, have credited miracles, unparalleled, latent, and awful: those very men, who rejected a public fact, often predicted; with its type and proof before their eyes, in the person of Lazarus, in the son of the widow of Nain, and in the daughter of Jairus?

They fancied, they had seen a spirit; *Thomas will not believe, unless he put his fingers in the print of the nails,*[1] and Jesus appeals to their senses; *Behold my hands and my feet, handle me and see.*[2]

Shall we now be told that he was forced to invoke the

---

[1] John xx. 25.   [2] Luke xxiv. 39.

witneſs he impugned? I will not charge my adverſary with folly.

Read our Lord's language after the ſupper : *I will not drink henceforth of this fruit of the vine, until that day when I drink it new with you in my Father's kingdom :*[1] it was the fruit of the vine, not his blood : again, he ſays ; *this cup is the New Teſtament in my blood:*[2] is the cup properly a New Teſtament? and if not, is it an image?

Moreover, Chriſt uſed a figure, not only in giving the cup, but in giving the bread ; *This is my body broken for you:* his body was then broken, either literally or not ; ſo Sir, he ſaid ſtrictly ; *this is my body;* and abruptly attached the figure to the letter : *my body, broken for you*—verily ; aſtute-neſs is a great bleſſing, but we ſimple ſouls believe, that the bread is Chriſt's body, in the ſame ſenſe that his body was broken.

Fourth. It is paſſing ſtrange, that theſe literaliſts reject the natural, and exact our conceſſion of forced figures : a figure in the words ; *he broke the bread and gave it,* ſince he

---

[1] Matt. xxvi. 29.   [2] Luke xxii. 20.

gave his body under the femblance of bread; a figure in thefe words; *this is my body,* as the bread was not his body, until he had uttered thofe words; a figure in this; *my body, my body broken for you,* as his body was not broken on the eve of his paffion; a figure, in the injunction, *do this in remembrance of me,* from which no fane man can infer a facrifice of the Lord's body.

We meet a figure in the term *cup,* as applied to its contents; a figure, when he calls it *the New Teftament:* a figure, in ftyling it, *the New Teftament in his blood;* a figure; that *his blood was poured out for the remiffion of fins,* before it was fhed; a figure, in giving the cup; *I will not drink henceforth of this fruit of the vine;* and a figure, when he adds: *when he fhould drink it new in his father's kingdom.*

Gracious God—are thefe the men, who fpurn a figure in the words of the inftitution?

Spectatum admiffi, rifum teneatis amici?

Fifth. No lefs fore to this unerring Church, may be the proof, that her letter is violent and ftrained.

The tafk is eafy, by fimply fuppofing the word *this,* fo to ſpeak, a prefix of the bread, uſed by our Lord, when holding that, which he had taken, and broken, and ſaying, *this bread*, to refer to the bread.

Who will ſay that the phraſe, *this is my body*, is ſtrictly true? that bread, a lump of grains, is properly a ſtructure of blood, bones and nerves?

Let us hear in behalf of the letter, the claims of the pronoun to a divorce from the noun.

However jarring may be the views of our Latin brethren : ſome, holding with Bellarmin, that our Lord intended, *this*, to imply, *under this ſemblance, here is my body :* others, *this bread is i. e. will be my body :* all are ſhocked at the quibbling which perverts its obvious, natural and literal ſenſe, to a notion, figurative, obſcure and fanciful.

With effrontery no leſs offenſive, than the oſtraciſm of ſenſe, and reaſon, they cloſe the ſacred canon, abounding in metaphor, and lacking a ſingle term ſerving their theory.

A falſe poſition now drives them both from image, and letter to ſenſeleſs jargon.

To your candor we ſubmit the iſſue.

Thus runs the *figure*—this bread, a type of my death till my coming is my body, myftically and virtually.

The *letter;* this bread is my body, properly, and literally.

The *fubtlety* or logic, if any, thus far, is confined to the faid pronoun, which I affume, covers the bread.

It is the logic of the eyes, and common fenfe, the logic of the difciples, and of every donee of bread, whofe donor, in the act of fimple transfer, fo joins that pronoun with that noun.

The letter, now involves utter confufion : we muft admit the bread, in a ftrict fenfe, to be body of Jefus Chrift ; while confcious that the bread is not his carnal body.

Who now needs the fuccor of fubtlety ? let him fay, who claims *two diftinct fenfes for that pronoun, one, tranfient, allied to the fubject before the change, i. e. to the bread: the other, fixed, qualifying the attribute after its utterance, but that the two* this-es *do not differ, becaufe both exprefs the fame idea.*[1]

Verily Sir, are not thefe fneerers at our fhelter of meta-

---

[1] Perp. de la foi, tom. ii. lib. ii. chap. 11.

phyfics the firft to feek, and moft in need of it? do they
realize that unlefs our complaifance invefts this pronoun with
a novel function, favoring much of being *got up for the nonce*,
they muft admit the metaphor, or charge Chrift with duplicity?

Our Author argues, that the ordinance has two afpects;
this, which is bread, at the prefent inftant, *is*, my body, at
the next.

In the abfence of precedent, he fancies what our Saviour
might have faid, in turning the water of Cana into wine.

The phrafe, *this is wine*, pending a change, he thinks may
intend, *this which is now water, is wine at the next inftant;*
the argument, which he terms *executory*, forces the prefent,
to embrace two tenfes: he applies it to Aaron's rod, which
became a ferpent, and to Lot's wife, transformed to a
pillar of falt.

No one doubts, that had Mofes faid, pointing to his rod:
this is a ferpent: the words would fairly imply: *this will be
a ferpent;* or that at the doom of Sodom, *this is a fea of
Sulphur*, might fairly exprefs, *this will be forthwith a fea,*
which he is pleafed to call *a virtual, and operative propofition.*

Whence it ſeems, that all his logic reſolves in the dictum of his Church, that the verb *is* unites the preſent and the future.

Should he abandon the letter for the figure, we claim a hearing for our figure; and though he may tangle ſubtlety with ſubtlety, and ſtill more groſſly, add inſult to inſult, *this*, that I give you and have broken, *this bread is my body properly and literally*, is the only literal ſenſe, that can attach to the words of the ſupper.

We hold, that the clauſes, *this is wine; this is a ſerpent; this is a ſea of ſulphur;* if found in Scripture, ſhould be governed by the context: as in the phraſe *a tree is a man*,[1] we ſee no change, but a ſimple trope, imaging the tree as a warrior, or an element of power.

A charge of undue notice, againſt the figure, recoils againſt the letter, for which no warning is claimed.

The caſes are parallel; we will not grapple with ſhadows; we inſiſt, that it is more natural to believe, that

---

[1] Deut. xx. 19.

our Lord ordained an emblem of his broken body, under the name of his body; than that he changed the loaf into his fleſh : that it is leſs natural, to conſtrue his words, as *operative*, than as typical, even as the diſciples viewed the bread of afflietion, the paſſover and the chalice.

To this iſſue, I challenge all my opponents' acumen, but not his cant, and verbiage.

Will this champion of the faith deny that the Euchariſt is a holy ſign? it is the ruling of his Church—will he deny that the Euchariſt ſhadows Chriſt's body, dying, and nailed to the Croſs? let Rome anſwer; eſcape is vain, at every turn, metaphors ſwarm his path.

Can his labored rules of language, *his operative propoſitions*, his unreal ſhapes, his double duty of the pronoun, or his deſperate theſes avail him?

He makes but three points—

𝕿𝖍𝖊 𝖎𝖓𝖈𝖎𝖉𝖊𝖓𝖙𝖘 𝖔𝖋 𝖙𝖍𝖊 𝕴𝖓ſ𝖙𝖎𝖙𝖚𝖙𝖎𝖔𝖓—

𝕴𝖙𝖘 𝖓𝖆𝖙𝖚𝖗𝖆𝖑 𝖎𝖓𝖙𝖊𝖓𝖙—

𝕻𝖗𝖊𝖏𝖚𝖉𝖎𝖈𝖊—

He gains nothing by thoſe *incidents*, plunged in trope and myſtery; nor yet, from the *natural force* of the words, be-

cauſe to the diſciples, unwarned of a latent change, the darkneſs of the letter, was ample notice of the figure : *to prejudice*, only, can we refer the letter with its endleſs ſhifts.

We fault Rome, with treaſon to her intellect ; to the
analogy of the faith ; to the word of God : we ſhow that
ſubtlety is confined to her ſchool, that Our Lord taught his
diſciples, that he ſhould be no longer with them as an object
of expenſe ; but never even in the pangs of parting, promiſed his veiled humanity on earth.

We ſhew that Paul conſtantly calls the Eucharist bread ;
nay, while urging its claims to reverence : that the diſciples
adopted, and every incident implied the metaphor, which the
Papal Church admits in the Cup.

We define ten bold figures in the words of the ordinance :
we ſhew that its uſe was enjoined, as a token of Chriſt's
broken body, an obvious image ; and its letter, to be ſenſeleſs, revolting and monſtrous.

Sir, with wiſdom, and learning, you have common ſenſe ;
the ſafeſt guide to truth and duty.

I am, &c.

Letter Third.

 ULL of ſolemn emphaſis is the language of Cardinal Richelieu ; " proteſtants are impious, if they do not adore what they ſhould, and we are idolatrous if we adore what we ſhould not." The worſhip of the Elements, preſcribed by Rome, is a yawning chaſm to the hope of fuſion : we charge it with

Temerity :
Diſobedience :
Abſurdity :
Impiety : and
Superſtition.

Temerity.—This is not the cant of controverſy ; God is my witneſs, that the ſeverity of truth forbids milder terms.

The Bible reveals the eſſentials of Salvation, with divers matters of minor moment, but neither Prophet, Evangeliſt, nor Apoſtle has even alluded to Euchariſtic homage ; a ſilence, that would alarm me if in fellowſhip with Rome.

Would God thus prove our faith, and humble our hearts ? I am willing to ſurrender my reaſon, if he requires the ſacrifice: I will adopt any doctrine he teaches, but I am not chargeable with contumacy until ſhewn his precept.

You will find that ſacred truths are preſſed, in the ratio they bear to the needs of faith and practice.

Chriſt's glory is magnified ; *he is our mediator; the light of the world; the life; the truth; the brightneſs of his father's glory; he was from the beginning; he was God; he thought it not robbery to be equal with God; he made the world; the periods of time; creatures viſible and inviſible—he ſuſtains and governs all things, and his years ſhall not fail.*

Hence it is, that all the Angels of God adore the divine Saviour ; and that every knee ſhould bend at the name of Jeſus, the only name by which we can be ſaved.

Omiſſion in the narrative of the ſupper finds no apology in its brevity ; they who ſtate that Jeſus ate the Paſſover with his diſciples, in a large upper chamber, ſwept, and made ready, would not ſlur a vital fact.

Mark the preciſion and harmony of the Evangeliſts ; *Jeſus Chriſt broke the bread; when he had given thanks, he gave the bread to his diſciples, he charged them to do this in memory of his paſſion; after this, they ſung a hymn ; and then they went to the mount of Olives :*[1] a racy minuteneſs for a church, conceding the muteneſs of Scripture in ſo grave a matter.

It is noteworthy, that the hiſtory of the Inſtitution is both our model and rule ; the intent being clear from the mandate, *do this in remembrance of me ;* and from the text of the Goſpels, quoted, *totidem verbis,* by St. Paul.

Diſobedience. If this recital is a Chriſtian manual, he who deviates from the leſſons of our Lord on the eve of his death, is guilty of temerity, and contumacy.

How do you know, aſks Rome, that Chriſt was not adored at the ſupper ?

We reply, that every incident repels the faɔ : the diſciples neither recognize a myſtery, nor his entry into their ſtomachs, nor vary their recumbent poſture, a cuſtom of the

---

[1] Matt. xxvi.　Mark, xiv.　Luke, xxii.

period, and inapt for the act of worſhip: they riſe only, to go to the Mount of Olives; and they ſtyle the Sacrament, the breaking of bread; that the early Chriſtians not only broke the loaf with marked ſimplicity, but gave it to the laity, to carry to the ſick and abſent.[1]

In view of theſe facts, it will appear not only incredible, but impoſſible, that either the diſciples of Chriſt, or of the Apoſtles, could have ſo adored the body of our Lord; and moreover, there being no record of the fact in that hiſtory, which has all the force of law, or elſewhere, and as Chriſt directs us to do in his memory, as he did with his diſciples, and St. Paul enjoins it—we hold that ſuch homage tranſcends his teachings.

Abſurdity. Our opponents brave both the ſacred Canon, and common ſenſe; their loyalty to either, would be a ſource of conſolation: we diſmiſs their vague maxims, claiming precedence for myſtery over the lights of reaſon, with the queſtion; if the human reaſon which condemns their dogma, is ſanctioned by the Holy Spirit; ſhall we try concluſions with God?

---

[1] Juſtin Martyr, Narrative of.

Read Sir, the Prophets on the vanity of idolatry : hear
Iſaiah—*they laviſh gold out of the bag, and weigh ſilver in the
balance and hire a goldſmith ; and he maketh it a God ; they
fall down, yea, they worſhip.*

*They bear him upon the ſhoulder, they carry him and ſet him
in his place, and he ſtandeth ; from his place ſhall he not re-
move ; yea, one ſhall cry unto him, yet can he not anſwer, nor
ſave him out of his trouble.*[1]

Again, in the xliv Chapter : *he heweth him down cedars,
and taketh the cypreſs and the oak, he planteth an aſh, and the
rain doth nouriſh it.*

*Then ſhall it be for a man to burn, for he will take thereof,
and warm himſelf ; yea, he kindleth it, and baketh bread ; yea,
he maketh a God, and worſhippeth it, he prayeth unto it, and
ſaith, deliver me ; for thou art my God.*

*They have not known nor underſtood for he hath ſhut their
eyes, that they cannot ſee, and their hearts, that they cannot
underſtand.*

*And none conſidereth in his heart, neither is there knowledge
nor underſtanding to ſay, I have burned part of it in the fire ;*

---

[1] Iſaiah, xlvi. 6, 7.

yea alfo, I have baked bread upon the coals thereof; I have roafted flefh and eaten it; fhall I make the refidue thereof an abomination? fhall I fall down to the flock of a tree?

Thus fpake the Prophet of idols ; and what think you of the apotheofis of pafte ; made of grains, ripened by the fun and rain, and cooked in an oven or between two plates of iron ; part of which, not from the hands of a goldfmith, but from thofe of a baker, is their daily meat ?

Can a prieft tranfmute this baked dough into a God, which they carry, becaufe he cannot walk ; which they lock up ; which they do not carry on their fhoulders, but in their hands ; which they put in his place, from which he cannot ftir ; which does not anfwer thofe who cry unto it ; part of which is ufeful to man, not to cook his food but as food ; which has eyes, but fees not ; ears, but cannot hear ; before which they kneel and pray, deliver me ; for thou art my God ?

Who will forbid us the indignant rebuke of the Spirit, and none confidereth in his heart ; neither is there know-ledge nor underftanding to fay ; I have made the half of this my bread, which I have cooked in an oven ; of the

refidue thereof, fhall I make an abomination? fhall I adore
a cake?

Can the Holy Spirit be fo foolifh, and falfe?—I fhudder as
I pen thofe words—would he pander to the mockery of Pagans?
Credat Judæus Apella, non ego.

If even the Jews, who afcribed God's prefence in their
groves and ftatues, folely, to the efficacy of their ritual,
fcorning the worfhip of mere wood and ftone, were branded
with idolatry, as faithlefs to inftinᵈt, will Rome exclude the
exercife of common fenfe, which Scripture exaᵈts? or if the
word of God denounces the fuperftition, that a tree the fruit
of fhowers, becomes a God; may we not judge the devotees
of fimple bread: which we have feen made of cereals by the
hands of a workman; do we err in reafoning like the Holy
Ghoft?

Impiety and Superftition.

If fuch homage is offenfive to God's fpirit; it is impious
and fuperftitious.

Many maintain, fir, and with much force, that if the
Euchariſt is material, Chriſt's body fhould not there be wor-
fhipped; unlefs vifible and glorious.

They diſtinguiſh between Deity, refulgent, and Deity, unſeen and ubiquitous: Rome attributes to Chriſt's humanity a dual ſynchronous preſence; as majeſtic; likened to the ſplendor of the firmament: and as veiled, in the guiſe of bread and wine.

Now, all Chriſtians concede that he who filleth immenſity ſhould not be adored in the trite objeɛts of nature, he is in a ſhrub, a rock; but the reverence allied with either is profane.

Chriſt teaches us to extol God in the ſtarlit depths of ſpace; as *our Father who art in Heaven;* becauſe, there, his eſſence is glorious: in paying divine honors to a tree, we might be ſuſpeɛted of deifying the tree, but who would imagine me worſhipping a ſtrange God; lifting my eyes to the golden garniture of the ſkies, which is the throne of God?

Be that as it may; they aſſume a truth which neither creed will queſtion; that Deity ſhould not be glorified in the frequent forms of matter, but in the grandeur of power.

Imagine the contempt, Sir; even of infidels, who watch you cold and tranquil, kneading and toaſting your wafer; and, *preſto,* bowing to your wafer God; and as you kneel in the mire before the Hoſt, will they not ſay, that you value Chriſt's cloaked humanity more than his Divinity; his body, more than his Spirit?

Jeſus Chriſt was adored, whilſt Deity ſhone in the incarnate God; when he huſhed the tempeſt; healed the ſick, and raiſed the dead; let us adore him, when viſible in his wiſe Providence, let us adore the Father, as throned in power; but do not inſult the majeſty of Jehovah; heap not blaſphemy on ſuperſtition, in adoring Chriſt's veiled body, ignoring his divine local and latent preſence.

If Rome changes the iſſue to a corporal preſence, in the nature of ſpirit; we repeat; why does ſhe honor Chriſt's body more than his Divinity?

If ſhe abandons the ſimple preſence, for that of grace; we reply, that in ſuch ſenſe, the Holy Spirit quickened the apoſtles, the cloven tongues at Pentecoſt, the hearts of Chriſtian converts, and in ſuch ſenſe animated the rite of baptiſm, without claim to objective worſhip.

The ark of the Covenant is not a caſe in point; before it, the walls of Jericho fell, before it the floods of the Jordan divided and cloſed behind it; there, God diſpenſed his living oracles to mortal ears; there was the Shekinah vivid between the Cherubim, thence called the Cherubim of Glory.

The ark was a *leſſer* heaven, evoking like emotions; verily, eyes have they, but they *ſee* not; ears, but they hear not; mean, and preſent in an atom : only preſent, at the pleaſure of a Prieſt; and not preſent, when the voided elements are dead and loathſome : all which we are told is the *crucial teſt* of faith.

That God's preſence in the ark was glorious, all admit: and Rome admits a glorious preſence of Chriſt only in heaven; in heaven, at the right hand of God, let us adore him, as he was adored in the ark.

And now, Sir, with all poſſible reſpect for my opponents, I aſk with Theodoret[1] *if it is not ſuperſtitious, and the chief of ſuperſtitions, to adore what we eat, or to eat what we adore?*

Is it not impious to worſhip that which the diſciples eat without change of poſture ; which ſight, taſte and reaſon pronounce bread ; which the Goſpel calls broken bread ; and of which, Chriſt enjoins no homage when teaching us to do, as

---

[1] Theodoret in Genes.—Ques. 55.

he then did : that which was eaten at the cloſe of a common feaſt ; which was freely ſent to the ſick and abſent by any applicant, and which, being a germ of the ſoil, cannot be God, ſave in defiance of his Holy Spirit.

Raſhneſs, folly, contumacy, blaſphemy and ſuperſtition are harſh terms for Roman cars ; I am loth to utter them.

Believe me, &c.

Letter Fourth.

Sir,

 GLADLY accept the iſſue, whether the diſciples could have regarded the bread as a type, without previous teaching.

It ſeems to me, that ſeeing our Lord take, break, bleſs and give the bread, they could have held many views more natural than the actual preſence or the change of ſubſtance.

I. The words, *this is my body*, would have recalled the paſſage of Deuteronomy, to which they are the key; *this is the bread of miſery that our fathers ate in Egypt.*

The ſenſes of the diſciples, their reaſon, the diſſonance of the bread and body; the nature of things; common ſenſe, all forbad the letter; but conceding the letter and the abſurdity of the figure; it is incredible, that they could or would have inferred a change of ſubſtance.

II. Had they wavered between what they ſaw, or ſuppoſed they ſaw, and heard, or thought they heard; it would have been more natural to miſtruſt their ſenſe of hearing, as we rely more on our eyes than our ears.

They knew by the ſight that the ſubſtance they received was bread; and they could only know by the hearing, that it was the body of their maſter.

Again, allowing equal weight to eye and ear, the perceptions of our direct viſion are more certain than the impreſſions we gather from the ſounds we hear; the diſciples ſaw the bread, but could only infer from the language of Chriſt, that the Euchariſt is his body.

Nor can it be ſuppoſed that the ear was ſpecially controlled by divine influence: its functions are free; by that channel only, I know that it is our Lord who ſpeaks; if the medium is falſe, it is untrue that he ſpeaks; if faithful, it is true; if doubtful, I may doubt if the Son of God ſpeaks.

The diſciples were more certain that they heard the words

of the inſtitution, than that the Euchariſt is Chriſt's body ; becauſe they believed it to be Chriſt's body on the credit of the hearing.

If they were equally ſure that they ſaw a real bread, and truly heard thoſe words ; they had a higher certainty that they ſaw a real bread, than that the Euchariſt is the body of Chriſt.

No one will deny that the diſciples had greater doubt that the Euchariſt is Chriſt's body, than that they heard his language : I hear Chriſt who tells me that the Euchariſt is his body, then the Euchariſt is the body of Chriſt, provided, the fact proved is more certain than the proof of the fact.

Nor will a certainty be denied to the ſight, at leaſt equal to that of the hearing, for if it is poſſible, that an object of our viſion is a mere ſemblance, it is more poſſible, that the ſpeech which we think we hear, may be deluſive found.

III. To the diſciples, lacking the training of the Propaganda, ſelf-diſtruſt was more natural, than abnegation of ſenſe, which their maſter had not impoſed.

A change of ſubſtance implies either, that the color, taſte and form before our eyes are not the color, taſte and form of bread, which is not pretended, or that all the accidents of bread remain after the bread has ceaſed to exiſt.

The ideas of ſpecies without matter; color without ſubſtance; bulk without body, are not eaſily graſped by men, who have not yet learned that what they ſee, is not what they ſee.

Could then the diſciples, like ourſelves ſubject to error—they who often miſtook their maſter's purpoſe and never when doubtful, ſcrupled to queſtion him—have adopted ſuch an anomaly in ſilence? and had they maſtered all his leſſons, could they without temerity and preſumption, have brooked a dogma, ſo monſtrous, even to conception?

IV. Be that as it may, folly only would deny a truce to Judgment, when the letter is offenſive to ſenſe and reaſon.

We read of the feet, hands, arms and eyes of God; of his approach; his preſence is manifeſt; he kindles the clouds with the fire of his breath, &c.—common prophetic images, ſuggeſting the funĉtions of a human frame.

Now, as reaſon rejeĉts the attributes of God to a body like Chriſt's, equally with corporeal faculties to Jehovah, and, as on no occaſion had the ſenſes and judgment of the diſciples been more ſtartled ; they could not have ſuppoſed, that their maſter's body, had, like God, a plural preſence, ſynchronous and latent.

But another view, and not without its force ; a plural pre-ſence not claimed even for God, is aſcribed to the body of our Lord ; in heaven and on earth, but not in ſpace ; and that his own body, with its bulk, unity, and proportions, was held in his own hand, and received into his own mouth and ſtomach.

Do we err in ſaying, that reaſon and common ſenſe revolt againſt the letter, and that then, if ever, Judgment would have been arreſted, or the ear ſuſpected, or firſt impreſſions rejected ?

V. The diſciples would rather have queſtioned the normal condition of their ſight, ſmell and taſte, a common event, than credit a diſguiſed change of the object of thoſe ſenſes ; and I inſiſt, that ſuch miſtruſt was more natural than the aſſumption, that the bread they ſaw was not bread.

VI. The words in queſtion, imply no leſs, that the bread is changed to the body of Chriſt, than that Chriſt is changed to the bread ; was it not then more credible, that inſtead of the bread, ceaſing to be bread, and becoming Chriſt's body, under the form of bread ; that the body of Chriſt had ceaſed to be his body, and the objeƐt that ſuffered death, was a ſemblance, the bread being his body by conſecration ? This ſenſe more natural than the tenet of Rome, abſurd as it is, would have ſaved the ſcandal of the croſs, ſo appalling to the diſciples.

VII. M. Arnauld, who doubtleſs makes the moſt of his caſe, thus conſtrues the ordinance : *This which is bread at the preſent inſtant, is my body at the next ;* in common par-lance, *this is about to become my body ;* the exaƐt letter of which will read, This bread which I ſhare and eat with you is about changing to the ſubſtance of my body, really, and ſtriƐtly ; being my food ; and this wine will ſoon blend with my blood, as it quenches my thirſt.

Had our Lord ſaid to his diſciples—eat this bread that I am eating, and turning into my fleſh, which muſt be broken for you ; drink this cup, that I am drinking, a fluid combining with my blood, that muſt be ſhed in ſanƐtion of the new cove-nant ; he would have implied that it was their laſt meal to-gether ; and that all was accompliſhed but the ſacrifice of his

body, fed by that food, and the oblation of his blood, aſſimi-
lating with the wine ; as he ſeems to expreſs it ; *I will drink
no more of this fruit of the vine, until I drink it new
with you, in the kingdom of God.*

We might further infer, that Chriſt gave his diſciples this
food, as a pledge, that his body ſhould be broken, and his
blood ſhed for their ſakes, as a communion with the means of
life eternal.

Here, is a rigid ſenſe, not reaſonable I admit, but leſs
ſhocking, and more tenable than the letter of Rome.

VIII. If the diſciples believed that Chriſt had but the
one body, which he ſtrictly promiſed to give them ; they
would have concluded, either, that he was guilty of a breach
of truth, which would be impious; or that the body of Chriſt
they ſaw being a phantom, the bread ſhould take his
name : the only eſcape from the conceſſion that the body
before their eyes, was the ſame that had entered their
ſtomachs.

IX. If the diſciples thought that Chriſt had a body which
extended its hand, and gave an object, and that Chriſt had a
body which they received from his hands, they could not

ſuppoſe that the Giver of the objeĉt and the objeĉt given were one.

To avoid the dilemma that one body was two bodies, or, that two bodies were one body, they had a fourfold choice.

That the body of Chriſt which extended the hand, had ceaſed to be his body, and had become bread.

That he, not the bread held out the hand, the ſame body, referred to in the inſtitution, and in the paſſage : *deſtroy this temple*, although the diſciples underſtood him to ſpeak of the temple at Jeruſalem.

That Chriſt had two bodies, the one giving ; the other given.

That the body of Chriſt which had been one, was duplicated.

They knew that two objeĉts, are two objeĉts ; they ſaw the ſubſtance given them by Chriſt, parting from his body, and without the aid of metaphyſics, could not have divined that the two were an unit.

X. The diſciples, unſkilled in the ſubtleties of the ſchools, and retaining their reaſon, would be wronged by the ſuppoſition that the language of the Ordinance, would convey the ſame ideas to them, and to the adroit logician: for, as no one would ſay, *here is the body of Peter, or here is his blood,* purpoſing to indicate the human nature of Peter; ſo, the diſciples, could not have inferred from the words, *this is my body, this is my blood,* the humanity of Chriſt veiled in the elements.

The literal ſenſe muſt be natural, and obvious: if then, in colloquial phraſe, *this is my body, this is my blood,* can only imply a body without ſpirit and blood without body; the diſciples muſt have ſo conſtrued the ordinance, if they adopted its letter.

The clauſe *my broken body,* was ſurely a metaphor, before Chriſt was actually broken, or crucified.

To cover this tender point, Rome reſorts to a ſubterfuge, tranſpoſing the paſt, and future, and even argues as if the word *broken,* were omitted.

We contend, that in the phraſes: *this is my body, this is my blood: body* and *blood* correſpond with *broken body* and *ſhed blood.* As it may not be ſaid of a body, or rather of humanity, *this is blood,* whilſt that humanity has a body, with blood courſing its veins, without braving every rule of diction.

The letter of the language aſcribed to Antony ; *the blood of the Roman Cæſar ſpeaks to you*, does not intend the perſon of Cæſar ſpeaking, but his blood free from his body ; and when Plutarch ſtates, that a ſlave found the body of Pompey on the ſhore, a vivid fancy, only, would infer, that ſuch body was living.

Back and fill as they pleaſe, *this is my body*, can never mean, *this is the living Chriſt Jeſus*, nor can *this is my blood* ever be referred to his humanity ; therefore, the body of Chriſt was a body, ſevered from its ſpirit, and its blood, was blood, parted from its body.

Now take the place of the diſciples, and aſk our Lord, what he enjoins us to eat and drink ?

Take eat; drink ye all of it.

Are we required to eat the bread ?

Are we commanded to drink the wine ? if we muſt drink his blood, how can we drink it properly while yet in his veins ?

You reply, that Chriſt does not exact an abſolute eating

and drinking, and why not ? If we adopt 'the letter of the inſtitution, why not the letter of the conjoined mandate, *eat, drink?* Moſt marvellous indeed, whilſt the Saviour ſays, *this is my body,* and ſtartled ſenſe and reaſon concede the figure, you inſiſt on the primary ſenſe, and when he naturally adds, *eat, drink ye all of it,* and ſenſe and reaſon demand a ſtrict compliance, you take refuge in the metaphor.

How can you properly drink the blood of Chriſt's veins, in the guiſe of wine ? the drinking of a ſeeming ſubſtance, is but a ſeeming drinking ; and a ſeeming drinking is not a proper drinking.

Pardon, Sir, this ſhort apoſtrophe to the infallible Church : and here let me aſk, what the diſciples could have underſtood, by a *body broken,* and by *blood ſhed* literally and properly : could they have regarded the Euchariſt as a bloodleſs ſacrifice, could they have conceived that Chriſt ſpake to them of aught ſave a dead body, and of blood from his own veins ?

XI. Nor can I ſee the virtue of a blind change which annuls the bread ; is Chriſt's body leſs free in ſubſtance, than in ſemblance ? if it can enter the form of bread, it can enter the bread itſelf; and if no exception is taken to diſproportion of the body to the bread, why ſhould the ſubſtance of one, be inconſiſtent with the ſubſtance of the other? in the ſilence of revelation, would not the modeſty of ignorance, be the foundeſt philoſophy?

XII. We will offer two hypotheſes; both clearly falſe:

That the diſciples were bound by the letter; and, that Chriſt's words, admit of no other literal ſenſe than that of Rome, which I aſſure you is a ſtretch of courteſy.

Had the diſciples been ſharply ſchooled at Port Royal, the notions of *preſence viſible,* and *latent; entities, actual,* and *ſacramental; unreal forms; converſions,* and *occult miracles* might have occurred to them; but they were poor fiſhermen, bleſſed with common ſenſe, nothing more.

Had they been philoſophers; they might not have fathomed in a breath, all the ſubtleties that Rome has needed centuries to deviſe; and had they diſcerned all thoſe niceties, even by grace; it ſtill is poſſible, they were not free from doubt.

Tortured as they were by fear, and ſadneſs, a ſuſpicion of

deluſion, or delirium would have ſeemed more natural, than the letter, ſubverſive of all their experience : it being more ſuppoſable, that the minds of a few men may be diſturbed, than the abiding convictions of all men are falſe.

If the diſciples were ſatisfied, that one and one, make two, that the whole is greater than its part ; or a veſſel greater than its contents ; that a human body, without loſs of bulk, is greater than a point, or that a ſubſtance, cannot properly and literally ſever from itſelf ; I contend, that a conceſſion of the marvels of Rome would belie every element of conſciouſneſs.

Imagine them taught, that the body which they ſaw, was the food they were eating, that Chriſt held his own body in his own mouth and hand, and gave himſelf from himſelf with his own hands, ſtill keeping himſelf to himſelf, or that his entire body, was taken into its own ſtomach, and with its full members, and proportions exiſted in the bread, and in each crumb of the bread, and was ſevered from itſelf, when they parted from their maſter.

We are told, that theſe are ſeeming flaws—but ſeeming— Gracious God—how far, is patience a virtue ? dare they tell me that the diſciples would not have ſpurned an hypotheſis which outraged their life-long convictions ?

There is no eſcape ; they muſt abide by the ſtern letter of every paſſage of Scripture, without the exerciſe of reaſon, or abandon their dogma.

And how may I aſk, do the Roman Scholiaſts conſtruc the paſſages—*a tree is a man ;*[1] *that rock was Chriſt ?*[2] "the letter is barred by common ſenſe."

Pauſe, Sir, while I apply that anſwer to the words, *This is my body ;* or *this bread is my body ;* if the pronoun is aſſignable to the bread ; is there more affinity between the bread, and the body, than between the tree, and the man ? prejudice apart ; what could you charge againſt my ſerious averment, that a tree is a man, that would not recoil againſt your letter ?

Hence, I infer, that the diſciples would rather have doubted their conception, or wakefulneſs, nay, even their reaſon, than harbor a doctrine involving abſurdity.

XIII. In fine Sir, I contend, that it is as natural, and

---

[1] Deut. xx. 19.   [2] 1 Cor. x. 4.

reaſonable, to ſink in Pyrrhoniſm, as to accept a ſenſe, which entails a doubt of our ſenſes.

Call to mind, Sir, that thoſe ſenſes ſuſtain the certainty of all our convictions; if falſe, our perceptions are falſe; if loyal; our perceptions are true; and our perceptions vague, if our ſenſes are treacherous.

If then, it is poſſible that our healthy ſenſes deceive us, in miſtaking the elements for bread and wine, we muſt regard their whole agency as fickle, if not as falſe; we muſt doubt the exiſtence of a heaven, an earth, and of our fellow man.

The Apoſtles could have fairly demurred to every proceſs of ſenſe: they who heard the preaching of the Apoſtles, with greater reaſon, ſhould have doubted their report of what others had heard or that which others had ſeen with their eyes, and which *their hands had handled of the word of life.*[1]

Let us traverſe the ſcale of confidence, acceſſible to the diſciples.

It is more certain that they ſaw Chriſt, than that they

---

[1] 1 Epiſt. John, i. 1ſt and 2nd.

N

truly heard him ; more certain, that they ſo heard, than that they underſtood him ; more certain, that they underſtood him, than that they adopted the letter, and rejeĉted the figure.

Again they were not leſs certain that they ſaw a real bread, than that they ſaw a real Chriſt ; ſince both faĉts have a common baſe—Ergo—It is much more certain as regards them, that the Euchariſt is bread, than that the Euchariſt is the body of Chriſt : to this iſſue, I invite all the ſubtlety of all the ſchools.

The reply, that the verdiĉt of the ſenſes is only true, *pari paſſu,* with the ſanĉtions of faith, is fallacious : firſt ; becauſe, it is ſenior of faith, and whether true, or untrue is independent—it is older than faith, becauſe the diſciples ſaw Chriſt, before they believed in him.

Secondly ; All our ideas of faith rely ſolely on ſenſe ; and their value to us, is meaſured by its certainty ; and to faith, which is a conviĉtion of Divine truth ; there are four eſſentials :

𝕲𝖔𝖉 𝖊𝖝𝖎𝖘𝖙𝖘 ;

𝕳𝖊 𝖎𝖘 𝖙𝖗𝖚𝖙𝖍𝖋𝖚𝖑 ;

𝔥𝔢 𝔥𝔞𝔰 𝔯𝔢𝔟𝔢𝔞𝔩𝔢𝔡 𝔥𝔦𝔪𝔰𝔢𝔩𝔣;
𝔈𝔞𝔠𝔥 𝔪𝔶𝔰𝔱𝔢𝔯𝔶 𝔬𝔣 𝔬𝔲𝔯 𝔣𝔞𝔦𝔱𝔥 𝔞𝔭𝔭𝔢𝔞𝔯𝔰 𝔦𝔫 𝔰𝔲𝔠𝔥 𝔯𝔢𝔟𝔢𝔩𝔞=
𝔱𝔦𝔬𝔫.

Sir—it is noteworthy—that the ſenſes are the ſole channels of all thoſe truths, and their ſole vouchers.

We are aſſured, that *there is a God*, from the wonders of the univerſe, which ſtriking our ſenſes, prove in the language of Paul, the divinity and power of its Author.

We believe, that *he is truthful;* being taught by the viſible creation, that he is too wiſe, to deceive himſelf, and too good, to deceive us : that *he has revealed himſelf*, by miracles, which have impreſſed our ſenſes, or the ſenſes of thoſe who atteſted them, with their blood and lives : that *each myſtery of our faith is found in Scripture*, becauſe our eyes have read, or our ears have heard it.

Thus the ſenſes, are the media of all evidence : if they cannot err, the grounds of your faith are firm—it is true, that we gaze on objeɛts, whoſe variety and grandeur proclaim the being of God : that we ſee marks of his wiſdom and love : that the eyes of ſix hundred thouſand witneſſes of the miracles of Moſes ; and the eyes of the diſciples who

certified the miracles of Chriſt, and the glory of his reſurrection; and the eyes of Chriſtians who for ages have read the
myſteries of their faith, have not mocked them.

Could our ſenſes delude us, all ideas of faith would be
unhinged: we loſe St. Paul's proof from the marvels of
nature, of God's exiſtence: ſuſpicious of all reality, we have
no conviction of his truth: doubtful would be the miracles
dependent on the viſion of others; doubtful would be the
myſteries, nay the fact of the written word.

I now offer ſome thoughts to the champions of Rome.

1ſt. As no geometric truth can ignore the axiom, *the
whole is greater than its part;* ſo, if faith relies on ſenſe, the
certainty of faith, being a concluſion, is ſubordinate to the
certainty of ſenſe; hence the certainty of faith cannot diſpute
the verdict of the ſenſes, that the Euchariſt is bread.

2nd. The evidence which proves is more clear, and concluſive to us, than the fact proved: now as the ſenſes under-
lie the truths of faith, our ſenſual aſſurance is more clear and
concluſive to ourſelves, than the truths of faith: conſequently,
the truths of faith cannot bind us to diſcard our ſenſes, which
affirm the Euchariſt to be bread.

3rd. The convictions of our normal ſenſes, are, either always falſe, or always true : or, ſometimes true, and ſometimes falſe.

If always falſe, we can never emerge from error : if ſometimes true, and ſometimes falſe, their report is dubious, and faith is unſtable, being a vaſſal of ſenſe : *Ergo:* the report of our ſane ſenſes is always true ; and that which my eyes pronounce bread in the Euchariſt, is bread.

4th. Common ſenſe demands the beſt evidence ; that of our ſenſes, ranks all evidence recognized ſolely through the ſenſes ; by their agency only, we know either him, or his miracles, his doctrine, or his miſſion—*ſequitur ;* although the authority of the ſpeaker may ſeem to imply that the Euchariſt is his body, the evidence of ſenſe, pronounces it bread.

5th. This dogma ſtrikes at the root of faith, which reſts on the teſtimony of the Prophets, of the Apoſtles, of Evangeliſts, of Martyrs, of God the Father, ſpeaking at the Jordan, and of Chriſt himſelf : all ſubject to ſenſe.

6th. If ſuſpicious of my ſenſes, I have no proof of the world's exiſtence : if uncertain of the world's exiſtence, I have no aſſurance that there is a God, who has revealed his will : if not aſſured that there is a God who has revealed his will, I cannot truſt either the ſincerity of the narrator, or even the fact of the inſtitution : if not convinced of the truth, or fact of the inſtitution, I am not bound to abandon my ſenſes, by adopting its letter.

Thus—*a primo ad ultimum:* I ſhould not ſlight my ſenſes in the matter of the Euchariſt, until ſure of their fidelity, which is amazingly cheering.

7th.   There is equal certainty in the two premiſes—*I ſee the Heavens, the Earth, the world: I ſee bread and wine in the Euchariſt.*

Equally clear, are the two concluſions : *the Heavens, the Earth, the world exiſt : the bread and wine exiſt.*

Nay, I have a firmer faith in the exiſtence of the bread and wine, than in that of the Heavens, becauſe, I only ſee the latter, while eyes, taſte, touch and ſmell, atteſt the reality of the former : however, aſſuming their equality, thoſe data afford a demonſtration.

I ſee the Heavens, the Earth, a world really exiſting, is clearer to me, than that *there is a God who revealed himſelf.*

The firſt being an axiom, the laſt, an inference ; now, the

term, *I ſee the bread and wine actually exiſting*, has the ſame clearneſs, force, and certainty, as the term; *I ſee the Heavens, the Earth, a world really exiſting.*

Therefore, we are more confident that we *ſee the bread and wine really exiſting*, than that, *there is a God who revealed himſelf.*

Can then the authority of God who revealed himſelf, require me, herein, to rule out the evidence of my eyes?

8th. There is a greater certainty, that *there was a perſon Chriſt who made the ſupper with his diſciples*, than that *the Euchariſt is properly the body of Chriſt*, and we have a higher conviction, that *the Euchariſt is bread*, than that, *there was a perſon Chriſt who made the ſupper with his diſciples;* in logical ſequence, we are more ſure, that *the Euchariſt is bread*, than that *the Euchariſt is the body of Chriſt.*

Surely, our conſcious certainty that, *there was a perſon Chriſt, who made a laſt ſupper with his diſciples*, is higher than the certainty, that *the words which Chriſt ſpake at the ſupper ſhould be rendered literally.*

That the Euchariſt is bread, is more clear than, that *there was a perſon Chriſt who made the ſupper with his diſciples,* ſince we learn the latter truth, only from teſtimony, but the former by viſion, our own eyes, being ſafer evidence, than the eyeſight of others, to ourſelves.

For Firſt—The diſciples ſaw their maſter diſpenſing the Euchariſt, and all ſee that the Euchariſt is bread.

Second—It cannot be denied, that at the ſupper, the diſciples were in ſore affliction, while we ſee the bread with tranquil minds.

Third—Our ſenſes, have no contact with the ſtatements of the diſciples, but teſtify directly, to the bread of the Euchariſt.

A truce to logic, as we track the ſhifts of bigotry.

Let us fancy a miſſion, to ſome Pagan race, to teach, the being of God, and the myſtery of the Euchariſt.

Suppoſe, they commune without comment, and after frequent partakings of the ſacred elements, which thoſe Neophytes believe, to be real bread, and real wine, you wiſh to undeceive them.

It is certain, on Roman theory, that their deluded ſenſes, miſtake for ſenſual food the body and blood of our Lord ; it is ſtill more certain, that you cannot ſurmount their prejudice.

Would you urge Chriſt's miracles ? As yet they know

him not : appeal to authority ? they recogniſe none : talk
of faith ?—talk to the winds : prove God's exiſtence and his
revealed will in the wonders of nature ? they will aſk you to
taſte, and ſmell the elements, and to prove them bread, and
wine, and your faith falſe, will require you to open your eyes
without reaſoning.

Would you preſs the lights of natural religion, and gently
lead to ſurrender of ſenſe, on the diſtum of Chriſt ? You
are again at fault, as thoſe men are void of common ſenſe, or
will refer your exaſtions to inſanity.

Hence it ſeems, that with ſound faculties aſting in healthy
concert and in their ſimpleſt funſtions, we are viſtims of ſelf-
deluſion.

If ſo—Adam could not and ought not to have been certain,
that he was eating forbidden fruit ; for if he was ſure that it
was fruit, the Pagans, we imagine, unwittingly eating the
hallowed bread, have like certainty of its reality, and if they
are capable of ſuch certainty, it is real bread, unleſs we may
be certain of that, which far from being certain is not even true.

If ſo, our firſt Parents might juſtly have queſtioned all they
had ſeen and all they ſaw.

If Adam could have doubted his ſenſes ; *à fortiori*, could Abraham have doubted, that he heard the voice of God, calling him to quit his country and kinsfolk : *à fortiori*, had Moſes cauſe of doubt, that God ſpake to him in Horeb : *à fortiori*, ſhould the Jews have defied their eyes when they ſaw the ſun ſtand ſtill to enſure the triumph of Iſrael ; when they ſaw rivers, changed to blood, and the terrors of the Exodus, rivalled by Pharaoh's jugglers : *à fortiori*, ſhould the Prophets have ſuſpected thoſe dim types, and parables, ſhadowing the counſel of God, their dreams, and viſions, of day, and night : their trances, their raptures, and thoſe multiform revelations, ſuſtained by evidence, ſubordinate to ſenſe : *à fortiori*, ſhould the Eaſtern Magi have ſcouted their ſenſes when their meteor guide ſtood over a child, whoſe manger cradle, chimed ſo ill with majeſty: *à fortiori*, ſhould the diſciples, have aſſigned to illuſion, thoſe miracles of the Saviour, which infringed nature's laws ; for, if ever inclined to queſtion ſenſe, it is not in matters of bread, and wine ; but in marvels, that awe the ſenſe, and challenge the reaſon.

The beacons of Rome ſtrand us on the quickſands of

doubt ; in fancied ſacrifice to faith, ſhe hazards the bulwarks of faith ; hazards, did I ſay ? ſhe rends the fortreſs, and up-roots its baſe; inſenſible to ſatire or ſhame, ſhe ſanctions the atheiſt's ſcoff, nay, poiſons the infidel's ſhaft, and ſtultifies herſelf, in blaſting the keyſtone of faith.

Our wayward mother muſt pardon our zeal for the ſenſes, which as witneſſes for the univerſe, warn us to be jealous of their rights.

I have now ſir, to apologize for the haſte of theſe letters, in behalf of their matter, which I claim to be concluſive.

I have expoſed the hazards of truth, tampering with duplicity, and of craft, and arrogance, being ſnared by their own devices.

The partizans of Rome may boaſt an able defence of a bad cauſe : God in his wiſdom, ſuffering an era, brilliant with eloquence and genius, to taſk its giant energies in clouding truth, that attrition of intellect might ſhed freſh luſtre on his holy faith.

I may ſeem bold, to enter the liſts with ſuch ſtalwart foes ; but while thoſe proud Philiſtines, are defying the armies of the living God, may I not hope, though as feebly armed as the Shepherd warrior of Iſrael, to confound them with a ſingle blow?

In my own cauſe, I would deſpair; but I am fearleſs in thine, O God, *who out of the mouths of babes and ſucklings haſt perfeɛted praiſe.*

I am, &c.

Notes to Translator's Preface.

 Reed.

Atteri et frangi fidelium dentibus.

Council of Rome, 1st Seſſion, A.D. 1059.

Collectio Regia : tom. 25, p. 592.

De latere effuſus eſt.

6, Council of Rome, A.D. 1079.

Collectio Regia : Rom. Coun.

4 Lateran 1215, capitula 1.

Summa conciliorum, tom. 1, p. 296 B.

Sub ſingulis, ſeu particulis—una cum anima et divinitate.

Conc. Trid. 13th Seſſion, A.D. 1551.

Teſt of faith.

Summa conc. de fide catholica, tom. 1. p. 296.

The Church decrees that all who neglect to receive the

Euchariſt at Eaſter ſhall be excluded from the houſe of God when living, and deprived of Chriſtian burial when dead.

Butler cites 21 Lateran—Cat. Leſſon 21.

Semper, &c.

St. Vincent de Lerens, 5th century commonitorium cap. 2. Milner, end of Con. p. 179.

Appeal to Scripture.

Butler's Cat. Euchariſt Bellarmine, Arnauld, &c. &c.

Jeſt.

Hocus pocus—hoc eſt corpus—&c. &c.

Merits of Saints.

St. Dominic did penance for others—the canons ſtated the terms—to wit : ten years for a homicide : a man guilty of many murders, being precluded by death ; St. Dominic by commutation, completed an hundred years with 20 chaplets and flagellation in ſix days : he thought that during Lent, he could accompliſh one thouſand years.

Fleury, A. D. 1062, lib. 60, ſec. 52. Paris, 1758.

This treafury entrufted to the Pope, confifts of the merits of Chrift, Mary and the Saints.   Pope's Bull, 1825.

Charlemagne was invoked as a Saint, miracles were performed at his tomb 250 years before his canonization : he had four queens and five morganatic wives in thirteen years. Fleury takes much pains to fhow a poffibility that he had not two at the fame time.

Fleury, A.D. 814, lib. 46, fec. 9.

Charlemagne was canonized 29 Dec. 1165, by an Antipope (Pafcal III.) ; the honor approved by the Pope.

Fleury, A.D. 1165, lib. 71, fec. 22.

Pierre d'Abre—Inquifitor, flain by the populace,for cruelty ; was made a faint by Paul III. *at requeft of Charles V.*

Vol. 24th Fleury, A. D. 1485, lib. 106, fec. 16.

Purgatory.

The council of Trent enjoined *found doctrine* in the matter of Purgatory *without defining it.* The Benedictine editors admit that the fathers not only differed from each other on this fubject, but that each was not confiftent with himfelf : Conc. Trid. 25th Seff.

Benedic. Ed.   St. Ambrofe I. 385.

It is the pious opinion of illuſtrious men that ſouls do not ſuffer in purgatory on Sunday, but return to their puniſh-ment on Monday. The maſs in honor of the angels is cele-brated on Sunday to propitiate their mediation for the dead and dying.   Fleury, A.D. 1062, vol. 13, lib. 60, ſec. 54. Council of Florence—

Purgatorium ignem eſſe.

Souls are purged from venial ſin by fire and the prayers of the prieſts ; mortal ſins by eternal fire—(if not diſpenſed ?)— *Queſtio de igne purgatorio.*

     4th June, A.D. 1438. Collec. Regia, de Purgatorio,

         Summa conciliorum, tom. 1, p. 396.

     Purgatory—confirmed at Trent—25th Seſſion, A.D.

         1563, Summa conc. tom. 1. p. 588.

Immaculate conception.

This dogma ſeems to have been broached in the 12th century. John Duns (Scotus) formally introduced it in 1307—he ſuſtained the poſition, that the conception of the virgin by her mother, was immaculate, by 200 arguments before the univerſity of Paris.

Fleury, A. D. 1308, vol. 19, lib. 89, ſec. 28.
Chal. Dic. Duns.

St. Bernard condemned it as a *novity* unſuſtained by authority of Scripture, reaſon or tradition.

Fleury, A. D. 1140, vol. 14, lib. 68, ſec. 70.

In the liturgy of St. Baſil the virgin and ſaints are prayed
for. St. Baſil, Op.

Anterior to A. D. 1307, both Franciſcans and Dominicans
oppoſed this doctrine—the Franciſcans changing their faith
conteſted the point with the Dominicans. The former
offered proof by miracles, the latter quoted Scripture and the
Fathers. F. Paul, Trent, A. D. 1676, p. 170.

The Council of Baſle recommends the obſervance of the
feſtival of the conception, not as an article of faith, but in
compliance with uſage. 36 Seſſion, A. D. 1439.

A. D. 1546, Paul III. directs the Council of Trent not
to meddle with it. F. Paul, 171, Trent.

About A. D. 1845, the Pope collected by letter the views of
the biſhops, of whom 40 are known to have diſſented—and
made it a part of the Roman creed, and a condition of
ſalvation.

The Biſhop of Arras, France, in his Paſtoral, A.D. 1867, expreſſes himſelf forcibly, *Satan howled in hell, when the doctrine was proclaimed.*

Pſalter of Bonaventura, Genoa, A.D. 1606.

Come to her all ye that are weary and heavy laden and ſhe ſhall give you reſt.

Chriſt ſays, *Come to me all ye,* &c.   Matt. xi. 28.

There is but one mediator between God and man—the man, Chriſt Jeſus.   1 Tim. ii. 5.

Bleſſed are the paps which thou haſt ſucked—yea, ſays Chriſt, *rather bleſſed are they that hear the word of God and keep it.*   Luke xi. 27, 28.

St. Paul aſks prayers for himſelf.

       2 Theſs. iii. 1.   Hebrews xiii. 18.

       1 Theſs. v. 25.   Romans xv. 30.

Efficacy of the Supper.

The views of the fathers, ſchoolmen and Roman divines are collected by Archbiſhop Tillotſon. Some of them are noted below. Calixtus—publiſhed at Helmſtadt—is the beſt authority, as the object of his life was to effect a comprehenſion of the Calviniſts, Lutherans, and Romans.

2nd Century—*Tertullian*—The firſt Latin father whoſe works are extant. " The bread is his own body, that is, the figure and image." Ad Marcionem I. 4, 571. Edit. Paris, 1634.

" If we doubt our ſenſes, we may doubt whether our " Savior was deceived in what he heard, ſaw and touched : " he might have been deceived in the voice from heaven, in " the ſmell of the ointment at his burial, and in the wine at " the ſupper." Lib. de anima, p. 319.

3rd Century—*Origen*—The higheſt name in Church hiſtory.

" The bread is Chriſt's typical or ſymbolical body."

Edit. Huetii, Commonit. on Matt. xv.

Cardinal Perron ſays that " here Origen talks like a heretic."

3rd Century—*St. Cyprian*, to Cecilius, Ep. 63, " by wine the blood of Chriſt is figured."

4th Century—*St. Auguſtin.*

" The elements are the figure and ſign of Chriſt's body " and blood. Our Lord does not doubt to ſay : this is my

" body when he gave the ſign of his body."

Tom. 6, p. 187. Edit. Baſil, 1596.

Speaking of Judas : he delivered to the diſciples the figure of his body.   Enarat, 3rd Pſalm.

Tom. 8, p. 16.

Commonitorium, 98 Pſalm. Ye are not to eat this body which you ſee, &c. the ſacrament ſpiritually underſtood will give you life.   Tom. 9, p. 1105.

Speaking of his body : ye ſhall have me according to grace but not to the fleſh.   Tract 50 in Joan.

The term, Sacrament, implies that from reſemblance, things take the names of things they repreſent.

Tom. 2, p. 93, 23rd Epiſtle.

As we receive the ſimilitude of his death by baptiſm ſo may we alſo receive the likeneſs of his fleſh and blood : that neither truth may be wanting, &c. quoted by Gratian de conſecrat. dis. 2.   Sec. utrum.

4th Century—*Theodoret.*

Chriſt honored the ſymbols with the name of his body and blood, not changing nature, but adding grace to nature.

Dialog. 1.

They remain in their former fubftance. , Dialog. 2.
5th Century—*Gelafius*—Pope.
The facrament ceafeth not to be the fubftance or nature of
bread.   Adv. Eutych. et Neft. fec. v. pars 3.
Biblioth. Patrum, tom. 4.

6th Century—*Facundus*—African bifhop.
Bread not properly his body, p. 144. Edit. Paris, 1676.

13th Century—*Scotus* Duns ; until the Council of Lateran,
1215, it was not neceffary to believe the doctrine of Tranfubftantiation.   In Sent. 1, 4, dis. 11, 9, 3.

15th Century—*Tonftall;* before the Lateran Council—the
manner of the Eucharift was a matter of opinion.

De Eucharift. 1, p. 146.

16th Century—*Erafmus.*—It was late before the church
defined Tranfubftantiation unknown to the ancients, both
in name and thing.   In 1 Epis. ad Corin. c. 7.

16th Century—Cardinal *Cajetan.* Card. of Leo X.
There is nothing in the gofpel that requires the belief that
the words of Chrift, *this is my body*, are to be taken in a
proper fenfe.   In Aquin. 3rd part, c. 75, art. 1.

Mem. This paffage is expunged in the Roman edition by

order of Pius V.   Ægid.—conſid. ſacram. 21, 75, art. 1, n. 13.

16th Century—*Fiſher*, Biſhop of Rocheſter.

In the words of the inſtitution, there is not one word from which the true preſence of the fleſh and blood in the maſs can be proved.   Contra Cap. Bab. c. 10, n. 2.

Seventh Ecumenical Council.

Great, holy and univerſal, held by Conſtantine V. with 338 Biſhops, including the moſt eminent prelates in the Church : the miſſion church of Rome was not repreſented.

                    Col. Regia, tom. 17, p. 591.

At the 2nd Council of Nice, the ſeventh Council of Conſtantinople was denounced as *mendacious calumniators of Chriſt : the council* of *Iconoclaſts*.

The church claim 377 biſhops preſent—better opinion, 318.   6th Seſſion, 6 Oct. A.D. 787.

                    Vid. Collectio Regia.

                    Sacroſancta concilia, tom. 8, p. 1046.

Images muſt be *adored* with relative affection, reſerving to

God the higher worſhip of Latria : unanimous. 2nd Seſſion of 2nd Nice, 27th September.

God does not prohibit the worſhip of manufactures.

Sacroſancta concilia, tom. 8. p. 759.

The text of this decree in the Roman authorities is an afterthought. Seven years after ſecond Nice, the Council of Frankfort, called by Adrian I. A.D. 794, charges that Council by its ſecond canon *de adorandis imaginibus*, with anathematizing all who do not worſhip images with the ſame adoration as the Holy Trinity. Eginhartus pretends that it is not the Council of Nice that paſſed the canon that Frankfort condemns, becauſe it is called by Frankfort the Council of C. P. ; Fleury, more honeſt, although his conſcience is galled by ſuperſtition, not only aſſerts the fact, but leaves Adrian with the ſtain of ſubterfuge.

It is well known that the ſeventh council of C. P. was not held at Conſtantinople, but at Hieres in Aſia Minor, and only ſo called from its proximity to C. P. Nice, modern Iſnick, is but ſeventy-five miles ſouth-eaſt of C. P. It is not ſuppoſable that the fathers at Frankfort, many of whom no doubt were at ſecond Nice—the matter public and recent—

would have condemned that canon—diſregarding Adrian's denial that ſuch canon exiſted—without an official knowledge of its text.

Conc. Francofordienſe, Col. Reg. tom. 20, p. 149.

Fleury, A. D. 794.

Paſcaſius.

Paſc. *ad Frudegardum.* Paſc. admits ſubſtantially the novelty of his doctrine.

Ratram, 12mo. Latin and French, 1686—he wrote this treatiſe by order of Charles the Bald, and dedicated it to him.

John Scotus—Erigena—his works were condemned at the council of Verceil, but not until 200 years after they were written.   Fleury, A. D. 859, lib. 49, ſec. 51.

Scotus was a ſaint for many years—Baronius ſtruck his name from the calendar—as unſound on the Euchariſt.

Archbiſhop of Mentz, better known as Rabanus Maurus, Abbot of Fulda.   Epis. ad Heribal, cap. 33.

Berenger.

Council of Rome, A. D. 1059.

Ego Berengarius, &c. non folum facramenta, fed in veritate manibus facerdotum, tractari, frangi, et fidelium dentibus atteri —alfo *relapfe* of Berenger. Collec. Regia, tom. 25, p. 592. *6th Council of Rome,* February, A.D. 1079.

De virgine natum—in cruce pependit—corpus in dextra Patris fedens effe, in proprietate naturae et veritate fubftantiae.

Judicious Omissions.

Tractari and *frangi fidelium dentibus,* are excluded from Berengarius' fecond confirmance of the faith.

Collec. Reg. tom. 26, p. 588.

The carnal theory of the Eucharift has been a fource of chronic agitation to the Church. The minorite Friars, A.D. 1371, under the leaderfhip of John de Laune, raifed teft queftions with fanatic zeal.

If the hoft falls in a foul place or is eaten by a beaft, is Chrift thereby elevated to Heaven? or does he pafs into the ftomach, or does the bread refume its nature?

St. Thomas held that the bread, once changed to the body and divinity of Chrift, could not be reftored to its cereal nature. Viclefqui in England, contra; Gregory XI. would

not take the reſponſibility of deciding : at the ſuggeſtion of
the grand Inquiſitor, he declared all excommunicate who
ſhould entertain the queſtions.

Fleury, A. D. 1371, lib. 97, ſec. 21.

𝔐anner of the 𝔈uc[bariſt.

Verona's ſubſtitute " to accommodate the views of both
partics."   F. Paul. C. of Trent, lib. 4, p. 309, 310.

Edit. Lon. 1676.

Sacros. cons. tom. 20, p. 611.

𝔏ibertp of 𝔈onſcience, &c.

Encyclical Pius IX. A. D. 1864.

𝔄rtificial 𝔗enors.

Pius IX. ſuſpends this practice during his reign : he is a
rare inſtance of perſonal purity in the papacy. Antonelli
has machiavellized the Pontiff, who commenced his career as a
Reformer. There are many exemplary prelates in America,
among whom Biſhop McCloſky is eminent for capacity and

private worth. The clergy of Cuba and Mexico have not yet felt the effects of the Reformation.

Baptifm of Bells.

Now fo common, was forbid by the capitular of Charlemagne. Fleury, A.D. 789, lib. 44, fec. 46.

The Diet of Nuremberg, A.D. 1518, condemned the practice as fuperflitious, its object being to drive away tempefts and devils. Recently at Montreal 2 bells were baptifed, one named Marie, the other Edward Albert Louis, with godfathers and godmothers.

Indulgences.

Trent, 4th December, A.D. 1563, 35th Seffion.

All are anathematized who deny this power to the Church.

Summa concil. tom. i. p. 598.

The world moves.

Galileo.

13th Century. Roger Bacon the philofopher was imprifoned fix years by the General of his order (Francifcan) on charges like to thofe againft Galileo.

Uera Crux.

The monks of St. Medard had a milk tooth of Chriſt. At Laon they had the milk of the Virgin.

Fleury, A. D. 1124, lib. 67, ſec. 36.

At the recent deſtruction of the convents of Mexico, Dr. Navarro, now Conſul General from Mexico at New York took ſome of the relics, bones of ſaints—to the family of Preſident Juarez; when broken they proved to be papier maché, made of muſic paper, lines and notes ſtill diſtinct.

Honor and veneration to relics.

Trent 35th Seſſion.

Summa conc. tom. i. p. 588.

Fruits of Sanctity.

Miracles are ſo-called.   Miracles were performed by falſe relics at Dijon.   Fleury, A. D. 844, lib. 48, ſec. 21.

Sacrifice—hoſtia.

Hoſt,—victim or ſacrifice. The maſs continues the ſacri- fice of Chriſt.   But. cat. Euchariſt.

Ultimatum.

More martyrs have been burnt for rejecting this doctrine than for difbelief in any other.

Pliant.

A. D. 597—Gregory I. inftructs St. Auguftine to accommodate the ceremonies of the Church to heathen rites.

Chalmers Dic. Aug.

Henry of Liege, nearly allied to the Duke of Brabant, confecrated Bifhop before he was Prieft, was guilty of crimes not fit to repeat : *he was advifed by the Pope to be converted and not to truft to his youth.*

Fleury, A. D. 1273, lib. 86, fec. 27.

Benedict XII. promifed Petrarch a difpenfation that he might retain his benefices, if he married Laura.

Fleury; A. D. 1374, lib. 97, fec. 33.

Alexander VI. grants a difpenfation to Ferdinand of Naples, to marry his own aunt, a child of 13.

Fleury, A. D. 1495, lib. 118, fec. 75.

Clement XI. inftructs his miffionaries to fuit Chriftianity to the liking of the Emperor, and incorporate Chinefe ceremonies in the ritual, A. D. 1700.—Life of Claude.

The Roman Church has a difcriminating difcipline (known as the policy of imitation) for every country. She would hefitate to trammel the Bible in the United States—as fhe does among more fubmiffive nations.

The Maronites—originally monothelites, protected by Emperor Heraclius—are now incorporated in the Church of Rome—their priefts marry—fervice in Arabic—mafs in ancient Syriac.

The United Greeks eftimated at two millions are united to Rome with refervations : their Priefts marry—facrament in both kinds : Greek fafts, and liturgy in Greek.

Unchurched.

The Patriarch of Antioch with advice of Patriarch of Conftantinople, excommunicates the Pope and the whole Roman Church for perfiftent fimony, ufury and many other errors.   Fleury, A. D. 1238, lib. 81, fec. 11.

Ignored by the Britifh Church.

The Reverend R. W. Morgan in his learned work—*St. Paul in Britain* proves beyond doubt that the Anglican

Church received her creed from the lips of the apoſtles.

Catena authoritatum.

Clemens Romanus, co-laborer with St. Paul: Tertullian, 2nd century—Euſebius, 3rd century—Chryſoſtom, 4th century—Theodoret, 5th century—&c. &c. &c.

St. Paul preached probably in both Greek and Latin. Cæſar ſtates that the Greek was known to the Druids.

Mr. Morgan makes a probable caſe from the undeſigned chronology of hiſtorical fragmenta, that Chriſtianity was firſt introduced into Britain by Joſeph of Arimathea, A. D. 36— quotes the admiſſion of Cardinal Pole in Parliament A. D. 1555, that the Britons were the firſt to receive the Chriſtian religion. At that date Rome was Pagan.

It is now generally admitted that Conſtantine, and his mother Helena, were native Britons of the Royal blood, and there can be little doubt that the Eaſt was more indebted for purity of faith to the Apoſtolic Church of Britain, than Britain to the Eaſt.

None but a lunatic would doubt, ſays Baronius, that Conſtantine and Helena were born in Britain.

Baronius ad. ann. 306.

Repudiated by Avignon.

From A. D. 1305 to 1377, feven Popes at Avignon—called by papal hiftorians the Babylonifh captivity of the Popes.

Their licentious lives provoked the Romans to expel them: ad interim, the Germans elected rival Popes at Rome.

Clement VII. at Avignon and Urban VI. at Rome excommunicate each other.   Fleury, A. D. 1379, lib. 97, fec. 61.

Pope againft Pope.

Stephen VII. A. D. 896, condemns his predeceffor Formofus—A.D. 891—has his body exhumed and brought into council, dreffes him in Pontifical robes, affigns him an advocate—calls on him to anfwer for his crimes—has 3 fingers cut off; the body thrown into the Tiber.   Col. Regia, tom. 24, 688.

Stephen is put in irons and ftrangled.

Fleury, A.D. 896, lib. 54, fec. 27.

Pope Sergius III. condemns Formofus.

Fleury, A.D. 906, lib. 54, fec. 42.

A. D. 963, Pope John XII. drives Pope Leo VIII. from Rome.

A. D. 972, Benedict VI. and Boniface VII. are rival popes. Benedict is ftrangled, Boniface ejected.

Fleury, A. D. 972, lib. 56, fec. 36.

A. D. 997, Gregory V. Pope. John XVI. Anti-pope.

A. D. 1118, Gelafius II. Pope. Gregory VIII. Anti-pope.

A. D. 1130, Innocent II. Pope. Anacletus II. Anti-pope.

A. D. 1159, Alexander III. Pope. Victor IV. Anti-pope.

A. D. 1164, Alexander III. Pope. Pafcal III. Anti-pope.

A. D. 1168, Alexander III. Pope. Calixtus. III. Anti-pope.

A. D. 1175, Alexander III. Pope. Innocent III. Anti-pope.

A. D. 1295, Boniface VIII. confines Ex-pope Celeftin V. in a cell about the fize of his body left he may elect to re-fume the Pontificate he has refigned—guards him night and day with 6 knights and 30 foldiers. Celeftin dies of cruelty. Boniface celebrates a folemn mafs for him at Rome. Fleury, A D. 1295, lib. 89, fec. 41.

A. D. 1389, Pope Clement VII. at Avignon, and Pope Boniface IX. at Rome, interchange excommunica-tion. Fleury, lib. 54, fec. 42.

A. D. 1463, Pius II. iffues a bull condemning his own books. Fleury, lib. 112, fec. 101.

Council with Council.

Second Ecumenical Council of Nice, repudiates ſeventh Ecumenical Council of Conſtantinople.   Col. Regia.

Council of Frankfort, called by the Pope, condemns the idolatry canon of 2nd Nice. See ante, p. 119.

Fleury, A. D. 794, lib. 44, ſec. 38.

The Council of Rome condemns the council held by Pope Formoſus ſame year. Stephen VII. Pope.

Col. Reg. tom. 24, p. 688.

Fleury, A. D. 896, lib. 54, ſec. 28.

The Council of Rome condemns the Council of Stephen VII. and ſuſtains Formoſus.

Col. Reg. tom. 24, 903, A. D. 896, Col. Reg.

Sergius III. A. D. 906 , condemns Formoſus and honors Stephen VII.

The Pope and Council of Ferrara excommunicate the Council of Baſle as ſeditious and contumacious.

Fleury, A. D. 1438, lib. 107, ſec. 79.

The Council of Baſle annuls the Council of Ferrara as ſchiſmatics and fornicators. 2nd Seſſion.

Councils with Popes.

Councils with Popes.

Council of Rome depofes John XII. for inceſt, murder, blaſphemy, and elects Leo VIII.

> Fleury, A. D. 963, lib. 56, ſec. 6 and 7.

John XII. with moſt of the ſame council who depoſed himſelf condemns Leo as adulterer and uſurper ; alſo condemns the council. Fleury, A. D. 972 to 975, lib. 56, ſec. 7.

Gregory VII. depoſed by the Council of Worms.

> Fleury, A. D. 1076, lib. 62, ſec. 28.

The general Council of Piſa denounces Benedict XIII. A. D. 1394, and Gregory XII. A. D. 1406, as perjured heretics. 15th Seſſion.

The Council of Conſtance depoſes Pope John XXIII. for deteſtable habits. Fleury, A. D. 1415, lib. 103, ſec. 59.

Pope Eugenius IV. equips gallies to fight the gallies of the Council of Baſle.

> Fleury, A. D. 1437, lib. 107, ſec. 44.

The Council of Baſle depoſes Pope Eugenius IV. as a perjured, incorrigible and dangerous heretic. 34th Seſſion.

> Fleury, A. D. 1439, lib. 108, ſec. 74.

The Council of Milan ſuſpends Julius II. in the name of

the Father, Son, and Holy Ghoſt, as hardened, contu-
macious and incorrigible.   8th Seſſion.

Fleury, A. D. 1512, lib. 122, ſec. 113.

Prelacy.

Gregory I.—St. Gregory—deſcribes the prelates as con-
cealing wolves' teeth under the faces of ſheep.

Fleury, A. D. 595, lib. 35, ſec. 39.

The moſt holy biſhops engage in war like the laity.

Fleury, A. D. 674, lib. 29, ſec. 50.

Battle and bloodſhed—murder at St. Peter's ; quarrel
between Pope and Biſhop.

Fleury, A. D. 864, lib. 50, ſec. 33.

Biſhop Athanaſius puts out the eyes of his brother, the
Duke of Naples, ſends him priſoner to Rome and uſurps his
Government.   Pope John VIII. praiſes the biſhop as loving
God more than his brother and plucking out the eye that
offended according to the precepts of the ſcripture.

Fleury, A. D. 877, lib. 52, ſec. 47.

Council of Mayence—Shocking inceſt of biſhops.

Fleury, A. D. 888, lib. 54, ſec. 2.

Some of the clergy live in open licentiou∫ne∫s.

Fleury, A. D. 956, lib. 55, ∫ec. 55.

King Edgar's addre∫s to the Council.

The clergy je∫t and laugh at ma∫s, are drunkards, gamblers, gluttons, wantons.

Fleury, A. D. 969, lib. 56, ∫ec. 30.

The Bi∫hops, bigami∫ts, drunkards, u∫urers, perjured, &c. —many of the clergy do not know the apo∫tles' creed—guilty of every po∫∫ible crime. Fleury, A. D. 974, lib. 56, ∫ec. 44.

Benedict VIII. forbids the clergy to have mi∫tre∫∫es— orders their children to be ∫laves in the churches where their fathers are prie∫ts. Fleury, A. D. 1022, lib. 58, ∫ec. 47.

The prelates dream of nothing but the gratification of their brutal pa∫∫ions. Fleury, A. D. 1394, lib. 99, ∫ec. 1.

The bi∫hop of Prague cau∫es a bi∫hop to be beaten and a prie∫t to be robbed and beaten.

Fleury, A. D. 1074, lib. 62, ∫ec. 10.

In convention at London, the archbi∫hop of York ∫its on the knees of the archbi∫hop of Canterbury; their partizans then fight with fi∫ts and clubs. King laughs : the legate adjourns the Council, *fine die.* Fleury, A. D. 1176, lib. 72, ∫ec. 58.

The Council of Ravenna condemns the conduct of the clergy as ſcandalous and contemptible—forbids the clergy to enter houſes of debauchery or bear arms.

Fleury, A. D. 1317, lib. 92, ſec. 37.

Debauchery the occupation of the clergy of Spain.

Fleury, A. D. 1473, lib. 114, ſec. 8.

Clergy often appear in public with looſe women.

Fleury, A. D. 1537, lib. 138, ſec. 31.

Bloody fights with fiſts and clubs between the Greek and Roman prieſts were common at the Holy Sepulchre at Jeruſalem until within a few years—the Turkiſh authorities interpoſed with force to reſtore peace.

Hierarchs.

St. Cyprian at the Council of Carthage charges the See of Rome with tyranny. Each biſhop is anſwerable only to God. Fleury, A. D. 256, lib. 7, ſec. 29.

Canon of John VIII. confirmed at the Council of Troyes: *no layman, unleſs deſired, muſt dare to ſit in the preſence of a biſhop.* 4 Seſs. Council of Troyes, A. D. 878.

Fleury, A. D. 878, lib. 52, ſec. 53.

Gregory VII. threatens to anathematize all France unlefs King Philip abandons fimony—the authority of Zachary who depofed the King of France, is given—Zachary alfo abfolved the French from allegiance.

Fleury, A. D. 1073, lib. 62, fec. 6.

Gregory VII. depofes and excommunicates Henry, Roman Emperor—abfolves his fubjects from allegiance—authorifes the election of another Emperor.

Fleury, A. D. 1076, lib. 62, fec. 36.

Gregory VII. depofes and excommunicates the Emperor of Germany—condemns him to be worfted in all combats—the anathema is in form of a letter to St. Peter, his brother Paul, and all the faints. Fleury, A. D. 1080, lib. 63, fec. 1.

Gregory VII. claims the right to fubject all the kingdoms of Europe to the Papacy—he claims moft of them as fiefs of St. Peter. Fleury, A. D. 1081, lib. 63, fec. 8.

Hildebrand—Gregory VII. was elected Pope by acclamation of the lower orders of Rome, and called to his aid the arm of fecular power—the act of canonical election is antedated to the day of his popular election *before Alexander was buried.* Dupin, Hildebrand.

Celeftin III. when crowning Henry VI.—kicks the crown
which he holds in his hands, to the floor, to affert his claim to
depofe Emperors.   Fleury, A. D. 1191, lib. 74, fec. 29.

Clement V. depofes John of England, and abfolves his
fubjects from allegiance—no one may eat with him or fpeak
to him under pain of excommunication.

Fleury, A. D. 1211, lib. 77, fec. 5.

The Council of Lateran with approval of Innocent III.
orders large numbers of heretics to be delivered to the fecular
power for punifhment—their property confifcated. Secular
officers muft fwear to chafe all heretics *pointed out by the
Church* from their lands—Thofe fufpected of herefy, after
one year to be condemned as heretics.

Fleury, A. D. 1215, lib. 77, fec. 46.

Gregory IX. excommunicates the Emperor Frederick.

Fleury, A. D. 1215, lib. 79, fec. 38.

The Pope repeats the anathema and abfolves the fubjects
of Frederick from allegiance.

Fleury, A. D. 1229, lib. 79, fec. 57.

Gregory IX. writes to St. Louis, King of France, that
God has confided to him imperial power over Earth and

Heaven—threatens him with excommunication—St. Louis
pays no attention to the demands of the Pope.

Fleury, A. D. 1236, lib. 80, ſec. 54.

The decrees of Councils where legates preſided prepared at
Rome—no one permitted to examine them.

Fleury, A. D. 1237, lib. 81, ſec. 7.

The Emperor's manifeſto ſtyles the Pope, the great
dragon that ſeduces the world, antichriſt, Balaam, the Prince
of darkneſs—German prelates ſupport the Emperor.

Fleury, A. D. 1239, lib. 81, ſec. 24.

The Pope after depoſing the Emperor of Germany, offers
the Empire to Count Robert, brother of St. Louis, King of
France. Fleury, A. D. 1240, lib. 81, ſec. 36.

Innocent IV. wiſhes to eſcape to England—the Engliſh
ſay—*we will not permit the Pope in perſon to rob the Church
and Kingdom.* Fleury, A. D. 1244, lib. 81, ſec. 17.

The Pope abſtracts more money from England than comes
to the hands of the King.

Fleury, A. D. 1245, lib. 82, ſec. 28.

Innocent IV. by Encyclical, dated 25th June, 1251, *in-
vites the heavens and earth to rejoice at the death of the*

Emperor Frederick.   Fleury, A. D. 1251, lib. 83, ſec. 25.
In proceſſion of the conſecration of Boniface VIII. the
King of Sicily holds the Pope's bridle, and waits on him at
table, wearing his crown.

Fleury, A. D. 1295, lib. 89, ſec. 35.
Julius II. excommunicates Louis XII. of France, and
offers his kingdom to the firſt who would ſeize it—he
marches at the head of his armies againſt the Duke of
Ferrara.   Fleury, A. D. 1510, lib. 121, ſec. 112.

Julius II. conduɛts the ſiege of Mirandola, rides over the
field—night and day in the batteries—points the cannon—
harangues the troops.   Fleury, A. D. 1511, lib. 122, ſec. 1.

Leo X. creates a cardinal aged eight years, on condition
that he ſhould not exerciſe his funɛtions until the age of
fourteen.   Fleury, A. D. 1517, lib. 125, ſec. 7.

Paul III. creates his two nephews cardinals—ages fourteen
and ſixteen.   Fleury, A. D. 1534, lib. 134, ſec. 162.

Pius V. excommunicates Queen Elizabeth as a rotten
member of the Church's body—ſlave of crime—monſtrous
uſurper—diſpenſes her ſubjeɛts from their oath of fidelity—
all excommunicated who obeyed her orders—Felton poſts the

bull on the houſe of the Biſhop of London. ⋅

Fleury, A. D. 1570, lib. 173, ſec. 2 and 3.

Sixtus V. excommunicates the King of Navarre.

Fleury, A. D. 1585, lib. 177, ſec. 33.

The King of Navarre poſts Monſieur Sixtus, the heretic, antichriſt, ſelf-ſtyled Pope—as a liar, on the palaces of the cardinals, on the houſes of Rome, and on the doors of the Vatican. Fleury, A. D. 1585, lib. 177, ſec. 35, 36.

Sixtus V. excommunicates Queen Elizabeth—*ſhe has not rendered homage for England as a fief of Rome*—offers a reward for the ſeizure of her perſon, that ſhe may be puniſhed for her crimes—he opens the treaſures of the Church to all who execute his orders.

Fleury, A. D. 1588, lib. 178, ſec. 32.

Sixtus V. excommunicates Henry III. King of France.

Fleury, A. D. 1589, lib. 178, ſec. 110.

Uicars of Chriſt.

Impious and infamous.

At the election of Damaſus—the two factions fight—137

dead bodies of men, women, and children found in the church beſieged by Damaſus.

Fleury, A. D. 366, lib. 16, ſec. 8.

Sergius III. having been elected Pope, A. D. 891, and exiled ſeven years, is recalled—he declares John IX. and Benedict IV. Leo V. and Chriſtopher, the three Popes following him, uſurpers.

Theodora, miſtreſs of Sergius III. abſolute in the Government of Rome—her two daughters, Maroſia and Theodora, leſs circumſpect than herſelf—Pope John XI. the ſon of Sergius and Maroſia, A. D. 931.

Fleury, A. D. 907, lib. 54, ſec. 42.

John X. is elected Pope by the intereſt of Theodora, his paramour.   Fleury, A. D. 912, lib. 54, ſec. 49.

John XII. elected Pope at the age of 18—grandſon of Maroſia and her huſband Alberic—raiſes troops and attacks the Prince of Capua—John XII. changes his name from Octavian: the firſt inſtance of change of name in papal hiſtory.   Fleury, A. D. 956, lib. 55, ſec. 50.

The Council of Rome condemns John XII.

1. He ordained a boy of 10 years a biſhop—ſimony.

2. He abuſed ſeveral women, one of them, the miſtreſs of his father—called inceſt.

3. He had made the ſacred palace a place of debauchery —alſo an incendiary.

4. He put out the eyes of his ſpiritual adviſer, reſulting in death.

5. He killed a cardinal, ſub-deacon, firſt mutilating him in a manner not proper to repeat.

6. He drank for the love of the devil and invoked heathen Gods.

7. He did not obſerve matins—neglected to make the ſign of the croſs.

The Pope does not deny any of the charges, but excommunicates the Council in the name of God Almighty.

Fleury, A. D. 963, lib. 56, ſec. 6, 7.

John XII. the above Pope is killed by a blow on the head in the commiſſion of adultery.

Fleury, A. D. 964, lib. 56, ſec. 10.

Benedict IX. aged 12 years, elected Pope by bribery—his life is infamous—reigns eleven years.

Fleury, A. D. 1033, lib. 59, ſec. 31.

Benedict IX. is driven from his palace for murder and other crimes.

Sylveſter III. becomes Pope—Benedict IX. returns to Rome with his forces and continues his exceſſes—ſells his pontifical rights to enjoy more licenſe in pleaſure, for 1500 livres to John Gratian who takes the name of Gregory VI.— *non obſtante*—the purchaſe and ſale—Gregory VI. Sylveſter III. and Benedict IX. all claim the Papacy.

Fleury, A. D. 1044, lib. 59, ſec. 47.

Leo IX. marches his army, collecting all the rabble he can enliſt, againſt the Normans—a bloody fight—the Pope is captured—he releaſes the Normans from excommunication as the price of his liberty. Fleury, A. D. 1053, lib. 59, ſec. 82.

Alexander IV. on his death bed orders the Inquiſitors to ſell the confiſcated property of heretics and apply the proceeds to the needs of the Church.

Fleury, A. D. 1261, lib. 85, ſec. 7.

Clement V. ſells his benefices—his miſtreſs is the beautiful Counteſs of Perigord—he ſpeaks of it openly—leaves immenſe wealth to *nephews*.

Fleury, A. D. 1314, lib. 92, ſec. 11. Villani.

Clement VI. licentious as archbiſhop and Pope—exceeds the young nobles in gallantry.

Fleury, A. D. 1352, lib. 96, ſec. 13.   Villani.

Innocent VIII. has ſeven children—different mothers— before his election—the exact ſums of money and names of the *Chateaux* given to the Cardinals to ſecure the election ſpecified—generous and courteous before his election—took for his motto *I will waſh my hands in innocency.*

Fleury, A. D. 1484, lib. 115, ſec. 142 and 145.

Corpſe of Innocent VIII. hooted with maledictions by the populace in defiance of military authority.

Fleury, A. D. 1492, lib. 117, ſec. 30.

Alexander VI. (Borgia) is elected Pope—his Holineſs is forthwith adored by the Cardinals : the croſs placed in the window : the prelates kiſs his feet : the young nobles have a torch light carouſal in the Place of St. Peter's and receive the approval of the Pope.

Alexander VI. has four ſons and a daughter: their mother is the wife of Dominic Arimano—his ſecond ſon, Cæſar, a cardinal.   Fleury, A. D. 1492, lib. 117, ſec. 31.

Alexander VI. ſeeks the aſſiſtance of the Turks againſt

the French.   Fleury, A. D. 1494, lib. 117, ſec. 90.

Alexander VI. in an attempt to poiſon four of his richeſt cardinals whoſe heir he is as Pope, poiſons himſelf and dies.

Fleury, A. D. 1503, lib. 120, ſec. 5.

Julius III. creates the keeper of his monkey, a cardinal.

Fleury, A. D. 1549, lib. 145, ſec. 156.

Julius II. Leo X. Clement VII. and Paul III. all believe in aſtrology.   Fleury, A. D. 1559, lib. 154, ſec. 32.

Sixtus V. feigns decrepitude : before the votes were fully counted, aſſured of his election, he flings his crutch into the middle of the hall, ſtands erect and looks like a man of 30, and ſings the *Te Deum* with a ringing voice.

Fleury, A. D. 1585, lib. 177, ſec. 22.

Sixtus V. in council applauds the zeal and courage of Jaques Clement, the murderer of Henry III.

Fleury, A. D. 1589, lib. 178, ſec. 121.

Shifting Creed.

The firſt Council of Nice A. D. 325, prohibits any additions to the creed (Nicene).

Cup.

A. D. 1195. The Council of Clermont decrees the communion in both kinds—28th canon—*nifi corpus, feparatim et fanguinem,* &c. Col. Reg. tom. 26, p. 663.

The Council of Conftance admits that the primitive Church communed in both kinds, but decrees that whoever fo communes is a heretic, muft be fubjected and punifhed.

Fleury, A. D. 1415, lib. 103, fec. 79.

The general Council of Bafle gives the Cup to the Huffites—*non obftante,* they declare it a herefy.

Fleury, A. D. 1436, lib. 107, fec. 14.

Twenty prelates of the one hundred and fixty-fix voting at the Council of Trent, favored the ceffion of the cup : there were fix conflicting views refpecting it.

Fleury, 1562, lib. 160, fec. 37.

The Cup was firft forbidden by the Latins A. D. 1300, although inftituted by Chrift, preached by the apoftles, and obferved by all Chriftian nations to that time.

Father Paul, Conc. Trent, p. 153.

Cardinal St. Angelo at Trent, would not give a cup full of fuch deadly *poyfon* to the people of France : it was better to let them die : the French ambaſſador did not think it right to give the name of poyſon to the *bloud* of Chriſt, nor that of poyſoners to the apoſtles.

Father Paul, Conc. Trent, p. 430.

Purgatory.

Unſettled until the Council of Florence 15th century— baſed on 2 Macc. xii. 46, Apocrypha.

See Butler's cat. purgatory.

Immaculate Conception.

Did not become a doctrine of the Church until the preſent century.

Tranſubſtantiation.

Penance.

A ſacrament by which venial ſins, committed after baptiſm, are forgiven.

Papacy.

Indulgences.

Conc. Trid. XI. 25, Butler's cat.

Mariolatry.

Infallibility.

The forged Decretals embracing the period from Clemens Romanus to Servitius, 300 years—pſeudo Iſidorian collection —for many centuries were law to the Church—although now allowed to be ſpurious, the Papacy clings to the material advantages of the fraud, to wit : the ſupremacy of the See of Rome, &c. &c.

Tradition.

Of equal authority with holy writ.

Butler's cat. leſſon.

Hail Mary.

The above ten and many other novelties were adopted after the prohibition of the firſt Council of Nice.

Two Natures of Chrifl.

The Neftorians were excommunicated A. D. 431, for holding among other views, two natures of Chrifl.

The Council of Chalcedon, A. D. 451, confirmed the doctrine of the two natures of Chrifl, which the Church had
repudiated.

𝔐angling and 𝔖hackling of 𝔖cripture.

Scripture was firft forbidden to the Laity at the Council of
Thouloufe, A. D. 1229—a Pfalter, breviary and hours of the
Virgin being allowed but not in the vulgar tongue.

Fleury, A. D. 1229, lib. 79, fec. 58.

ℭelibacy.

The power and crimes of Rome are all referable to the
confeffional and celibacy. If marriage be conceded to the
clergy, faid the Cardinal di Carpo at Trent—the priefts not
being dependent on the Pope, but on their Prince, the
authority of the Apoftolic See would be confined to the walls
of Rome.

The Roman Church calls celibacy, a holier ftate than that

from which Enoch was tranſlated, and impoſed by God on the high Prieſt of the Iſraelites, Levit. xxi. 14—and in which Abraham, the friend of God, lived—James ii. 23.

In 1 Timothy iii. 2, we are told that a Biſhop muſt be the huſband of one wife.

In 1 Timothy iii. 4 and 5, his children muſt be in ſubjection or how ſhall he take care of the Church of God?

In 1 Timothy iv. 3—*The Spirit ſpeaketh expreſſly that in the latter times ſome ſhall depart from the faith forbidding to marry.*

1 Timothy iii. 11—Paul inſtructs deacons how to chooſe their wives.

The bleſſed Virgin was married—Peter, *firſt Pope,* was married—all did well—thoſe who in times of perſecution were hiding in the clefts of the rocks did better to remain ſingle.

Terrific reaction.

Notes omitted.

Schiſm.

Vid. conflicts of councils, popes, &c.

Dominicans and Franciſcans—on immaculate conception—laſted many centuries.

Schiſm at Florence.   A. D. 1062.

Schiſm at Worms.   1076.

Schiſm during vacancy of Papacy after death of Celeſtin IV.—1 year and 8 months.   1241.

Innocent IV. a fugitive—no one will ſhelter him.   1244.

Papal throne vacant 2 years and 9 months ⎫
                                    ⎬ 1269-71.
Gregory X. elected by compromiſe   ⎭

Thomiſts and Scotiſts : efficacy of grace and imm. con.

Papal See vacant from death of Clement V. 20th April, 1314, to John XXII. 28th June, 1316.

Jeſuits and Janſeniſts on the doctrine of grace.

The hiſtory of the Church is a hiſtory of Schiſm.

Subterfuge.

Gregory VII. ſays that the Church has diſſembled many things which were ſubſequently adjuſted with great care.

                 Fleury, A. D. 1080, lib. 73, ſec. 7.

Gregory VII. claims that the Roman church has never erred.

Fleury, A. D. 1081, lib. 73, fec. 11.

Forged decretals—vid. ante, p. 147.

Corrupting canons—text of authors, &c. Vid. ante, p. 119.

Harbor of Slave Ships.

The ports of Spanifh Iflands are the only harbors of flave fhips.

It is now propofed in Spain to reftore the Inquifition.

Ireland.

Adrian IV. A. D. 1155, by bull authorizes Henry II. of England to reduce Ireland, to eftablifh pure Chriftianity, claiming all the Iflands profeffing Chriftianity as fiefs of the Church. He requires Henry to fubject the Irifh to the laws of England, extirpate their vices, and tax them a penny on each houfe as dues to St. Peter.

Fleury, A. D. 1156, lib. 70, fec. 16.

Previous to that time Ireland called the land of faints from the purity of her people.

In virtue of this fale or gift in A. D. 1169, an Englifh

army invades Ireland. In 1361, the province of Ulſter ſtill independent : In 1541 Henry VIII. whoſe title is Lord of Ireland under the Pope, is proclaimed King by the Iriſh Parliament—the iſland not conquered until 1603, by the invaſion of the Spaniards at the requeſt of the Pope.

Peter.

The papacy is baſed on Matt. xvi. 18—*Thou art Peter ; on this rock I will build my Church.* Proteſtants ſhow that Cyril, Jerome, Chryſoſtom, Leo I, Hilary, Ambroſe, &c, referred πετρα—rock—ſometimes to Peter, ſometimes to his confeſſion, ſometimes to Chriſt. St. Auguſtine in his *Retractions*, is ſatisfied that it applies only to Chriſt.

Peter as ſpokeſman of the Apoſtles, makes the firſt inſpired avowal of the Meſſiahſhip—Chriſt anſwers—thou art πετρος —Peter—a ſtone or piece of rock, and on this πετρα—rock— I will build my Church—not on the fleſh, but on the faith of Peter, or as Auguſtine hath it, on Chriſt himſelf—for we know that *the Church was built on the foundation of the Apoſtles and Prophets, Jeſus Chriſt being the chief corner ſtone* —Eph. ii. 20.

Our Savior ufed the word *keys* to defignate Peter's office as firft, to open the Church to Jews and Gentiles : fo Peter underftood it—Acts xv. 7.

In his difcharge of that duty he introduced the prefent policy of Rome—*imitation*—for which he was blamed by Paul and checked by the Council of Jerufalem.

No fupremacy was ever claimed by or accorded to Peter : on the contrary, at the Council of Jerufalem, Peter was defendant ; James as Prefident gave the decree commencing, *My fentence is*, &c, and alfo ruled againft the worfhip of images—Acts xv. 19, overruled by 2nd Nice which was again overruled by the Council of Frankfort.

Had Peter been Primate, no power was given by Chrift to his fucceffor—nor did Peter appoint a fucceffor, but inftructed the Prefbyters *not to be lords over Chrift's heritage*—1 Peter v. 3.

The fame power was given to all the apoftles to bind and loofe—to remit fins, &c.—John xx. 23. Matt. xviii. 18.

Moreover the ultramontane rock, not as bad as Judas, yet was moft exceptionable—the foolifh Peter walked on the water: the vengeful Peter cut off Malchus' ear : the Judaiſing Peter was withſtood by Paul to the face—the infidel Peter rebuked his maſter and received from Chriſt the name of Satan—Matt. xvi. 23—*vade poſt me Satana*, in the Vulgate. Satana is the proper Hebrew name of the Devil—ſo applied 34 times in the New Teſtament and only ſo applied, the word uſed for Satan in the wildernefs—Luke iv. 8.

The parallel of Peter with the Papacy fails with Peter's reformation; the offenſive Peter *that favoured not of the things that be of God, but of thoſe that be of men*—the faith-lefs Peter that after his confeſſion and boaſtful love, although forewarned and inveſted with the keys, denies his Maſter again and again, with curſes and oaths—denies himſelf—takes up his crofs and follows Chriſt.

Peter was never at Rome except by tradition—Paul wrote to the Romans calling many by name—he wrote ſix letters from Rome, but neither in thoſe letters, nor in the narrative of the *Aĉts* does it appear that Peter was ever there. There can be no queſtion that Peter was at Corinth—He wrote from Babylon, the See of his Dioceſe—thither no doubt, he led his wife, and there no doubt he died, after fulfilling the duties of huſband, father and biſhop.

Patrimony of St. Peter.

In the eighth century, all the Princes of the Merovingian family being imbecile, the Mayors of the Palace exercised royal authority over the Franks. Charles Martel held this rank at his death—his ſon and ſucceſſor Pepin, ambitious of the title of King, conſulted Pope Zachary who replied *that he ſhould have the name of King who had the power of a King.* Pepin was crowned A. D. 752, and confined Childeric III. King of France and his ſon, Theodoric, in ſeparate monaſteries.

Rome was attacked by the Lombards—Stephen II. preſuming on the credulity of Pepin, ſent him a letter in imitation of the Epiſtles—*Paul, called to be an Apoſtle of Jeſus Chriſt, Son of the living God, &c.* in which the Apoſtle Paul conjured Pepin in the name of the virgin, angels, martyrs, ſaints, to aid his ſpiritual mother and fight the Lombards, promiſing, if obedient, eternal ſalvation ; if contumacious, the penalties of hell.

Pepin, conſcious that his only claim to the Crown was derived from the Pope attacked and defeated the Lombards and gave to the Papacy as Patrimony of St. Peter 22 Lombard cities—whence arofe the temporal power of the Popes.

Fleury, A. D. 741, lib. 42, fec. 24.

„ 752, lib. 43, fec. 1.

„ 755, lib. 43, fec. 17.

„ 755, lib. 43, fec. 18.

Liberated Africans.

Paftoral of Rt. Rev. Auguftin Verot, Bifhop of Savannah, to Churches of Georgia and Florida, Sep. 1866.

Plenary Council of Baltimore, 1866.

Pius IX. is the only fovereign that conveyed his fympathy by letter to Mr. Davis during the Southern rebellion.

Letter of Bifhop Quinlan and others, of Mobile, to Pius IX. May, 1867.

Faithful Shepherds, &c.

Letter of Cardinal Barnabo— Prefect of the Propaganda. March 5, 1866.

Latin race.

Napoleon III. to General Forey—*Moniteur*, January 16, 1863.

Tranſlation of Papacy.

Pius IX.—allocution—Oɓober 31, 1866—If need be he will ſeek the freer exercife of his miniſtry in a foreign land.

Dec. 17, 1866—the leading Romaniſts of the Council of Baltimore invite the Pope by letter to viſit the United States.

The evident ſympathy for the Fenians in the Federal States is mainly due to their defiance of the Roman Church. —There is a recklefs tendency among American politicians to bid for popularity—The chief executive of the U. S. was confpicuous in the Plenary Council of Baltimore.

The ſame motive largely enters into the deſign of abforb-ing Mexico, Cuba, and Canada.

In the Roman *Ordo* of 1866, page 52—It ſeems that the *Hierarchy* in the United States is divided into ſeven Pro-vinces and five apoſtolic vicariates. Page 49, the *Hierarch* is John Mary Maſtai Feratti—crowned June 1, 1846, at Rome.

On page 64, the Biſhop of Axieren who ſucceeded the Biſhop of Baſileopolis has charge of the *partes*—infidel regions—*infidelium*—omitted here, but not omitted on page 53 —province of Oregon—-compriſing the province of New

York ſouth of 42 degrees north latitude, except Long Iſland.

On page 54, the Propaganda decides that the See of Baltimore has precedence in America—The Biſhop of Lingone, Baltimore, has a chancellor, and a council of 12 eccleſiaſtics.

Page 72, the Biſhop of Pompeiopolis lives *in partibus* at Cincinnati. The Biſhop of Claudiopolis has charge of the ſpace between 29th and 31ſt degrees of north latitude, which are not *in partibus*.

It does not appear by the Gazetteer that Claudiopolis, Pompeiopolis or Baſileopolis are cities in America.

Of the 310 churches in the City of New York, the Proteſtant Epiſcopalians have . 60

Preſbyterians . . . 43

Hebrews—Synagogues . . 26

Romaniſts . . . 33

Ritualiſts—St. Albans . . 1

In the United States the Papacy has Biſhops and Archbiſhops 47

The

Mitred Abbots . . . 3

Prieſts . . 2400

Churches 3671

Colleges, Schools and Academies . . 1500

Convents, ſtrictly ſo called . . 99

A large number of Monaſteries.

A.D. 1867, the Papal population is about 6,500,000 : in 1831, about 600,000.

Confeſſional.

Huſbands and fathers of daughters may conſult Sanchez to learn the queſtions authorized by the Church : and Dens, to learn the ſtandard of purity of the Confeſſor—Dens is a text-book at Maynooth. Liguori, a ſimilar *free* authority has been a ſaint fourteen years.

Jeſuit Peſtilence.

By Jeſuit ſtatiſtics publiſhed in Rome, February, 1865, the Society has 7,728 members, of which there are 726 in North America, 1 in Mexico, 28 on the continent of Europe out of the Roman States—In the United States they often

conceal the name of Jeſuit under ſome leſs odious deſigna-
tion.

Plague Spot.

Roman Catholic churches and inſtitutions, eſpecially thoſe
of the Jeſuits, largely depreciate values of Real Eſtate in
their vicinity.

The People of the United States now tolerate the Roman
worſhip ; the Pope excludes from the City of Rome, the
Churches of all creeds but his own.   What may Americans
expect if Rome ſhould gain the political aſcendancy at which
ſhe now openly aims ?   The American Proteſtant Chapel
within the walls of Rome has cauſed much contention—it is
however as yet unmoleſted.

The Papal Church in the United States has recently
adopted the title of *Roman Catholic.*   It appears in large iron
gilt letters over the gate of the Aſylum in 5th Avenue, New
York—*Roman Catholic Male Orphan Aſylum.*

Paſquin ever critical and claſſical has latinized the word
male, in dividing the ſyllables *ma* and *le,* by the point of the
gothic arch : an opinion, entitled to reſpect, traces this read-
ing, to a *Bull of Mileſius.*

𝕸𝖆𝖘𝖘𝖆𝖈𝖗𝖊 𝖔𝖋 𝕾𝖙. 𝕭𝖆𝖗𝖙𝖍𝖔𝖑𝖔𝖒𝖊𝖜.

25,000 butchered in the Provinces.

50,000 at Paris—the carnage continued a week.

See Fleury, Siſmondi, and Froude.

Charles IX. and his Court join the proceſſion formed to return thanks to God for the ſucceſs of the maſſacre—medals ſtruck to perpetuate its memory—Charles makes an ediɛt from the throne of *Juſtice*, that all had been done by his orders. Fleury, A. D. 1752, lib. 173, ſec. 35.

Gregory XIII. goes in proceſſion from St. Peter's to the Church of St. Louis, returns thanks to God, and ſtrikes medals in honor of the occaſion.

[A large painting of the maſſacre ſtill remains on the walls of the Vatican, a memorial of the Pope's gratification and approval—public attention is not drawn to it—although much obſcured by dirt, the antiquary may identify it by the inſcription.]

Philip II. of Spain attends the eulogium of the maſſacre. It is ſtyled *the triumph of the Church militant.*

Fleury, A. D. 1752, lib. 173, ſec. 39.

Philip is never known to have laughed during his whole life except at the announcement of the maſſacre.   Froude.

Charles IX. amuſed himſelf by ſhooting from the windows of his palace all that came within reach.

Prieſts with crucifixes and ſwords headed the murderous gangs, inciting them to kill friends and relatives.

ﬀarce of Trent.

The legates write to Rome that the inſtruƈtions of the Pope would make them the ridicule of the world.

Fleury, A. D. 1546, lib. 142, ſec. 41.

To ſecure a majority of votes, the Pope ſends back the Venetian biſhops who had left the Council for their homes.

Fleury, A. D. 1546, lib. 144, ſec. 11.

The papalins are abuſive: the merry prelates could not forbear obſcene jokes.   Father Paul—Trent, 598.

Henry II. of France for a long time refuſes to ſend delegates, as the Council is neither free nor general.

Fleury, A.D. 1551, lib. 146, ſec. 121.

Cardinal Loraine ſays the Council is not free, and its inſolency great.   Coun. Trent, Father Paul, 593, 594.

The chief legate enjoins ſecrecy on the fathers, leſt the world might know how little of moderation and harmony exiſts in the Council; many ſhed tears of ſhame, but conceal the faɛts until they become notorious.

Fleury, A.D. 1562, lib. 158, ſec. 74.

The Council is completely under the control of Pius IV.— this faɛt gives occaſion to the witticiſm of the French ambaſ-ſador, *that the Holy Spirit comes from Rome to Trent in a mail bag.* Fleury, A.D. 1562, lib. 159, ſec. 12, &c.

Pius IV. during the Council, orders the Inquiſition to cite Cardinal Caligni and ſeveral archbiſhops to Rome, to anſwer to the charge of favoring hereſy. F. Paul, Coun. Trent.

Curſed be all heretics.

Card. *Anathema cunɛtis hæreticis.*

Reſp. *Anathema—Anathema.*

The laſt words of the laſt general Council of Rome in the afternoon of Saturday the 4th day of December, 1563, A.D. 35th Seſſ. Collcɛtio Regia, Paris, tom. 35, p. 638.

Summa conciliorum, tom. 1, p. 600

The 255 delegates ſubſcribe under pain of excommunication.

The Cardinal of Loraine leads this acclamation with a voice of thunder: the hall ſhakes with the enthuſiaſtic reſponſe.

Cardinal Loraine entered the Council in the oppoſition, complaining that the Council was packed by tools of the Pope, and that it was neither general nor free : he was *conciliated* by Pius on his viſit to Rome at the Pope's invitation—Loraine had committed the acclamations to writing.— It was remarked that ſuch premeditated uſe of the word *heretics*, included the then preſent, paſt and future.

CHISWICK PRESS:—PRINTED BY WHITTINGHAM AND WILKINS, TOOKS COURT, CHANCERY LANE.